Theories of the
Capitalist Economy

Theories of the Capitalist Economy

Ben Fine
Reader in Economics, Birkbeck College, University of London

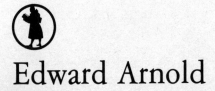

Edward Arnold

Copyright © Ben Fine 1982

First published 1982 by
Edward Arnold (Publishers) Ltd
41 Bedford Square, London WCIB 3DQ

British Library Cataloguing in Publication Data
Fine Ben
  Theories of the capitalist economy.
  1. Economics
  I. Title
  330   HB171

  ISBN 0 7131 6357

Filmset in 10/11 pt Garamond Compugraphic.
Printed in Great Britain by
Richard Clay (The Chaucer Press) Ltd., Bungay, Suffolk.

Contents

Introduction

The purpose of this book is to examine different ways in which theories of the capitalist economy have been constructed and to assess the merits and limitations of these various ways. As a result, its contents are intimately related to the history of economic thought since economists past and present are the most immediate breeding ground of economic theory.

The book is not intended, however, to be a contribution to the history of economic thought even over the limited scope of topics that it covers. For the history of economic thought, as part of the discipline of economics, has shown in general very little interest in discovering and questioning different methods of theorizing the economy. At times, the history of economic thought seems to be seen simply as an empirical exercise of intellectual investigation. The attempt is made to discover the extent to which a current theory or conceptualization is to be found in the past. It can be done with a greater or lesser degree of sophistication and rigour. To employ an exaggerated metaphor, at one extreme the archaeologists of economics reconstruct systems of thought in the light of modern theory. At the other extreme, letters, early versions of lectures and the ideas that they contain correspond to the cracked pieces of pottery that are to be dug up and restored. The history of economic thought becomes a test of 'primitive' economic theory for its conformity with modern economics. Those theories that fail the test are rejected, or more exactly, placed in the storerooms of the museum of academia. Those that do conform are exhibited in a place of prominence. Nothing may be learnt from such histories of economic thought about different theories of the economy, and by the same token nothing can be added to an understanding of the economy itself. The histories merely serve to confirm what is already deemed to be correct.

One of the main conclusions that we draw is that there have been very few, if any, new ideas in economic theory since the time of Adam Smith. We find that it is not so much discoveries that distinguish schools of thought as a differing organization of and emphasis on a recurring set of ideas, and sometimes the ideas excluded from a theory are quite as important as those included. In chapter 1 we attempt to analyse the ways in which ideas are incorporated into an economic theory by abstractions that have a social, historical, empirical and causative content that should be revealed in any assessment of the theory. In chapter 2, we examine the views of Smith and Marx on the division of labour. The division of labour as an object of economic analysis has become almost extinct and this is related to the simultaneous disappearance of a dynamic element in theory that is an intimate part of both Smith's and Marx's economics even if they do themselves differ. The significance of this element for Smith's value theory is taken up in chapter 5 and for Marx's theory it is implicitly reconsidered in chapter 8. Chapter 3 discusses Ricardo's theory of value and takes up Marx's critique of it. This is important since it is often assumed that Marx and Ricardo shared a labour theory of value in common. Also, in this chapter, a criticism is made of Sraffian interpretations of Ricardo's value theory. Sraffian critiques of neo-classical and Marxist value theory are well-documented (and contested), but the associated interpretation of Ricardo has remained relatively sacrosanct. We have attempted to question this sanctity. Chapters 4 and 5 complete the presentation of the value and distribution theories of Ricardo and Smith with each containing a critical evaluation of their implications. Ricardo's rent theory is confronted by Marx's critique and his alternative theory in which he shows the possibility of an absolute rent as a component part of price. This is itself shown in chapters 5 and 7 to be inadequately theorized by Smith.

The last three chapters are more concerned with modern economics. Chapter 6 contrasts the neo-classical with the classical school and attempts to explain the content of and reasons for the reaction against general equilibrium analysis during the early days of the marginalist revolution. Chapters 7 and 8 are concerned with topics that have become esoteric and are almost absent from orthodox economics today; that they have become so represents an important exclusion of ideas. In chapter 7 the decline of rent theory is examined and in chapter 8 the debate over the falling rate of profit is seen to correspond to the way in which dynamics are introduced into economic theory. In both of these chapters, the recent lack of orthodox contributions to the literature is significant and makes it necessary to make reference to less familiar sources. What literature does exist shows the difficulties that recent theory has in dealing with the problems and this is seen to be necessarily so by examining the contributions themselves. Finally the last chapter brings together the results of the previous chapters and examines their relevance for modern economics and modern economies.

The order of presentation within the book posed certain problems because of the possible use of two criteria for determining it. These are the views of particular writers or schools of thought to be set against views on particular subjects, such as value or rent. The first of these criteria has dominated but not exclusively. In particular, the presentation of Smith's value theory has been postponed to chapter 5 and is separated, by two chapters on Ricardo and Marx, from the chapter dealing with Smith on the division of labour. I felt this essential in order to demonstrate Smith's ability to construct an absolute component of rent and to contrast the role of competition in Ricardo and Smith.

All of the chapters in this book are my sole responsibility with the exception of chapter 8 which incorporates a shortened and slightly modified version of a paper written jointly with John Weeks. The majority of the book was written during the summer of 1980 whilst I was visiting the American University in Washington and is based on a course that I taught there and subsequently at Birkbeck College. I am deeply grateful and indebted to all those involved. Viv Brown, Martin Fransman and Laurence Harris commented on the first manuscript and this led to considerable improvements in the revised version.

Preparatory Reading

This book does presume a certain knowledge of economic theory, that may be obtained during a normal degree course. For a critical presentation of such material, the reader is referred to the two books edited by Green and Nore: *Economics: An Anti-Text* (1977) and *Issues in Political Economy* (1979). It also requires a limited knowledge of the history of economic thought including Marxist economics. The best source for this is the 'classics' themselves. To some extent this book can be considered a sequel to my earlier work *Marx's 'Capital'* (1975), which gives a simple introduction to *'Capital'*, *Rereading 'Capital'* (with Laurence Harris 1979), which reviews debates within Marxist economics, and *Economic Theory and Ideology* (1980), which contains an account of Sraffian economics, the labour theory of value and certain economic theories not covered in this book such as Keynesian and inflation theory.

Ben Fine   July, 1981

1
Towards a History of Economic Thought

On Method

There are different ways of approaching the history of economic thought. Perhaps the most popular is to assess the extent to which a theory anticipates the propositions of a current orthodoxy. Praise can be lavished on the doctrines of the past to the extent that they anticipate those of the present. Revolutions in economic thought can be seen as sharp breaks in a theoretical evolution, breaks that may or may not represent progress towards the current state of knowledge. Such an approach has serious limitations. It presumes the validity of the current orthodoxy and severely constrains the analysis of different schools of thought by this. The praise mentioned earlier is more by way of self-congratulation than critical evaluation. Further, by pursuing this method, the history of economic thought loses what is its most important function: to shed its critical light on modern economics rather than vice versa. Without this function it merely becomes an arid account of who said what and when, viewed through the filter of what is deemed to be important now.

Schools of thought in the past posed different problems, employed different methods and constructed different concepts than those used now. An assessment of them in an evolutionary retrospect is liable to devalue and distort their specific contributions by attempting to squeeze out of them what is not there (the elements of a theory of which they are not composed) and by neglecting what is there (the elements of a theory of which they are composed).

That different schools employ different methods does not imply that all theories are equally valid since they are all equally different. Nor that the historian of economic thought must adopt a pose of agnosticism to permit each school of thought a fair crack at the analytical whip. What is clear is that the historian of economic thought cannot confine himself to a narrowly defined economics since, quite apart from the philosophical basis of his economic method, economics as a discipline has included a social, political and moral content. A position must be taken on these if only to exclude them, as modern economic theory has frequently attempted to do.

In addition, agnosticism does not allow a debate with the economic theory under consideration, only a contrast and comparison. At best the agnostic could attempt to become a reincarnated Adam Smith for the course of a chapter or two and attempt to develop or reconstruct his theory by donning Adam Smith's thinking cap. He could even reconstruct a debate between a resurrected Smith and Ricardo. As an intellectual game this exercise might bear some fruit, but it could only be a disguised form of imposing the historian's head on Adam Smith's and Ricardo's.

The conclusion to be drawn is that the historian of economic thought cannot adopt a neutral posture and assess what are alternative theories as if he were an innocent bystander. The attempt to be neutral almost inevitably leads to an uncritical and unaware acceptance of standards by which economists are being judged.

What has to be recognized is that the historian of economic thought does adopt a theoretical position and that this can itself be debated as much as the theories under consideration and through the criticism of these theories. Thus the elements that we propose in the next section, that should be extracted from the various schools of economic theory as a means of understanding and criticizing them, are not to be accepted uncritically themselves. They have not been selected on the basis of arbitrariness and bias but with the justification that they will allow different economic theories to be comprehended in a way that adds to our own understanding of the economy.

The Elements of Economic Theory

In this section, we intend to discuss elements which will be present in all economic theories. However, how they are present and how they are combined with each other will differ and give rise to the differences between theories. We begin with the process of abstraction. All theory necessarily utilizes abstract concepts. This is not because the real world is so complex that more or less accurate assumptions have to be made as approximations although some theorists do look at abstraction in this way, as a making of approximately accurate assumptions. A prior consideration is that thought and its concepts are separate from the objects of the real world to be analysed. Theory can only reproduce the real world in thought. The concept of employment, for example, is not employment itself. So there is always a distance between the concept used and the part of reality it attempts to capture. This distance exists quite apart from how complicated a concept is. How this distance is to be bridged is a major philosophical question of some controversy and consequently how it is bridged in particular schools of economic thought is of considerable importance.

However, we do not wish to confront these problems directly here, but, having recognized the necessary difference between the real objects of thought and the concepts themselves, we can admit that the concepts have different levels of complexity. To return to the level of employment, this seems to be a simple concept. Closer examination proves this might be otherwise. Who is to count as employed? There are those employed in full-time and part-time employment, those paid wages and those self-employed, there are those whose employment appears outside the economy such as housewives and students. Apart from determining who counts as employed, the complexity of employment is illustrated by its composition. The employed are distributed across skills, trades, regions, sexes, etc. We can conclude that concepts that are simple contain the potential to become much more complex.

This raises the question of the relationship between the simple and the more complex versions of the same concept. It would be possible to allow the more complex versions to replace the simpler since they are more refined and seem closer to the complexity of reality. More generally, a more complex concept and the associated theory would replace a simpler one, the latter being considered a special case of the former. Such an approach is setting the theorist up for defeat. Since it is admitted that more complex theory is to be preferred to the less complex, any theory is presumed erroneous even as it is being put forward. It is open to the criticism that it could be further refined. It might appear that this is a desirable state of affairs since theory is in a state of permanent challenge, but it is a challenge that exists as the theory unfolds. Taken to its logical conclusion, the challenge would lead to an attempt to reproduce an exact replica of the real world in thought, for otherwise the theory would contain concepts that could be further refined. Within economics, this problem creates a tension between the atomised acts of individual exchange and the recognition of social categories such as labour or prices. We examine this tension in many of the following chapters.

The problem with the method outlined in the previous paragraph, quite apart from the general destruction it brings to all theory, is that it associates complex concepts with being more realistic and hence more desirable than simpler ones. We have already argued that all concepts are necessarily abstract even if some are simpler than others so that the realism or otherwise of particular concepts cannot be derived from whether they are more complex or not. There is a necessary divergence between the concept and the real however complex the concept, since no concept can be realistic in the sense of reproducing what is real other than in thought. What this suggests is that it is both possible and necessary for concepts to exist within theory at different levels of complexity, what is called at different levels of abstraction, but that this must be done in such a way that the simpler concepts are reproduced rather than displaced by the more complex concepts to which they have a relation. For example, if we have a notion of employment as the number of wage-labourers and subsequently theorize levels of employment in different sectors of the economy, our earlier simpler concept becomes redundant when our theory explains the level of employment as a whole by the independently determined levels of employment in each sector. It is simply a shorthand expression for numerical aggregation of employment across the different sectors of the economy.

If, on the other hand, our theory explains the overall level of employment as a whole and then argues that this determined quantity is distributed across the different sectors, then the level of employment as a whole has a different status than the sum of its constituent parts as defined in the earlier theory. It is a simpler concept than employment divided by sector but it is necessary for the explanation of the more complex concept. At the same time, we can observe that our second theory offers a different theory of aggregate employment than the first. It still requires a theory of the division of labour between sectors which does not contradict its prior proposition concerning aggregate employment. The second theory could also explain why the first theory would appear to be correct when it was not since the aggregate level of employment is formed from the sum of its individual parts although this does not necessarily cause it to be what it is.

In our view, all theory contains abstractions of the sort that we have outlined, that is the existence of concepts within the theory at different levels of complexity. As our example has brought out, this process of abstraction is related to a number of other properties of the theory. The most important is that theory develops relationships between concepts which are not simply logical in the formal or mathematical sense. The process of abstraction is one which builds up concepts quite apart from the numerical relations involved. To return to our example, the theory that explains the division of employment between sectors on the basis of a predetermined aggregate employment has started with wage-labour and would restrict the concept of employment to that wage-labour for which the theory holds, at the possible expense for example of seasonal and part-time employment.

The relationships built up are themselves complex. As we have seen, they involve reproducing simpler concepts at a more complex level and in doing so they produce other characteristics within the theory. One of these is the way in which explanation or causation is constructed. The existence of different levels of abstraction within a theory produces the idea that there are underlying forces at work which resolve themselves into more complex outcomes. Consequently a structure of causation is created within the theory in conjunction with the structure of abstraction. These two structures and the processes and relationships which are analysed to produce them are intimately connected but they are not identical. The most simple concept may not be the most fundamental in causation. For example, even if we accept the theory of a predetermined aggregate employment put forward above, it involves a notion of what is not included in employment and the unemployed or non-employed will have been defined by exclusion at the same simple level at which the employed have been defined. But they have been excluded precisely because they are to be shown to have a minimum causative significance despite their elevated status in abstraction. More generally, concepts which continue to have a causative significance for the theory may have a different status in causation than they do in abstraction. Another conclusion then that can be drawn is that both abstraction and causation do not constitute simple relations within the theory. For example, in much rent theory we shall see that the abstraction is made that the system of landed property has little or no effect on the determination of the level of rents. But the ownership of land does cause rents to be paid to whomsoever receives them.

Another result of abstraction has emerged from our example. Just as different concepts are imbued with a different status so they have a relationship which can be explained within the theory, to how things appear and how they are. Employment is the sum of the levels in individual sectors and this sum may appear to determine the aggregate level whether this is true or not. This distinction between reality and appearance, in which the latter is not entirely an illusion, is again related to the other properties of abstraction such as causation and the existence of simpler and more complex concepts. Overall then the abstractions that exist within a theory are liable to be extremely complex, containing many interrelated elements.

All theories contain the process of abstraction, but there are enormous differences in the abstractions that are made and the ways in which they are made. What all economic theory appears to have in common is a wish to come to grips with the movements of the capitalist economy. To do this concepts are drawn from capitalist society itself such as wages and profit, capital and labour. This use of concepts is as common to every economic agent as it is to the economic theorist. The individual capitalist does not stop to speculate over the conceptual content of profit. It is simply a question of getting on and maximizing it. Here the notion of profit is drawn from every day empirical experience. The modern neo-classical economist often reproduces these simple reflections of the businessman. But even if a more speculative approach is taken, an empirical content to the theory remains. Most obvious evidence of this is the reliance upon terms such as wages and profit which are grounded in a more or less direct contact with empirical observation and experience.

Accordingly, abstraction contains an empirical content. This content cannot be presumed to exist independently of the theory even if the relationships upon which it is based can be presumed to exist and appear independently of the individual. The simplest fact is open to varying interpretations according to the theory in which it is interpreted and incorporated. The empirical content of a theory then cannot be considered either to be a neutral starting point as in induction, nor to be the closing moment of verification as in positivism. The empirical content of a theory is precisely that: part of the theory.

As we have just seen, the empirical content of a theory can be introduced in many different ways and not just as a starting or closing point or both. It too will have a relationship to the abstraction within the theory and it can also be drawn from different sources. As mentioned, it can have its origins within the society under consideration, such as contemporary capitalism. Then a concept such as wages will have to be considered at different levels. Is it appropriate to analyse wages as a general average from which there are deviations to be explained or is each individual wage caused independently from the average, which is then a simple average of the individual levels with no other causative significance? Quite apart from the use of contemporary capitalism as a source of empirical material, an understanding may be drawn from historical analysis. Few would argue for example that contemporary capitalism is the same as nineteenth century capitalism because of monopoly elements. Nevertheless, it could be argued that contemporary capitalism is still best understood as if the market mechanism worked to create full employment equilibrium as suggested by the theory of competitive equilibrium. One presumption here is that nineteenth century capitalism is itself best explained by the theory of competitive equilibrium, but whether this is correct or not, the point is that contemporary capitalism is explained as if it could be identified with an earlier stage of development.

That this is possible follows from the existence in different societies of relations which appear to be the same. Prices, profits, wages, rent, labour and so on have an existence in many societies and so it becomes possible to identify them as being the same. Whether this is appropriate or not is a different matter. If feudal rent is used as a basis for explaining capitalist rent, the result is liable to be a misunderstanding of both. More generally, we can draw two conclusions. The first is that a theory will tend to bring together by abstraction from empirical material an understanding of a society or its economy by the use of concepts which have an applicability to one or more other societies. In an extreme form, this involves the use of general concepts that are applicable to all societies, concepts such as labour, production, technology and consumption. This should not be confused with the opposite process of treating a society in which a concept is inapplicable, such as profit under feudalism, as if it were applicable on the basis that feudalism has a surplus which might well be considered a profit, the form of a surplus under capitalism. In each case a conflation of different stages of development are utilized to produce the theory concerned. An example of this is given to us by neo-classical economics which is very much based on the idea that individuals are free and independent economic agents. Yet the very use of categories such as wages and profits suggests otherwise and that individuals are better understood in terms of their confinement within the class relations of capitalism. This is taken up in more detail in chapter 6.

Secondly, the incorporation of empirical material into a theory raises the question of how this is to be done. Money is money, but is money under feudalism identical to money under capitalism? Competitive prices may diverge from monopoly prices but to what extent are the two prices conceptually different and the same applies to the concepts of slave and wage labour? The question raises more general considerations, those concerning the validity of abstraction as it incorporates and develops a conceptual content out of its empirical one. An answer is suggested by raising two solutions at polar extremes. The first is to employ general concepts only. Then the result will be to create an analysis that has universal applicability. It will characterize every society and, because it has no specificity, it will explain none. It would be as if natural laws could explain social laws. At the other extreme, the empirical material incorporated could be so detailed that the analysis would be specific to a fleeting moment of time alone.

To strike a balance between these two extremes, a method has to be found which validates the use of concepts whilst at the same time limiting their applicability to particular periods of history. It is necessary to demonstrate that the theory reproduces in thought relationships which conform to the period of history to which they are applied. Now previously we have argued that theories contain abstractions which incorporate empirical material and notions of causation, but these abstractions may or may not have the property just discussed. For example, the neo-classical theory of general equilibrium used to describe the perfectly competitive economy utilizes the Walrasian auctioneer to set prices through *tatonnement*, so that all economic agents can be price-takers. But the auctioneer is a fictional product of the theory which therefore carries the unfortunate result that everybody is a price-taker so that prices are not set by anybody. Of course, it could be said that the economy behaves as if there were an auctioneer but a very simple deduction has shown that because there is not an auctioneer, the economy cannot behave as if there were one since no prices would be set.

In general then we do not find that the concepts used in economic theory are consistent within the theory itself with what the theory is attempting to study. This can be because of the construction of a fiction, as for the Walrasian auctioneer, or because of historical slippage, if feudal rent were to be explained as a profit for example. This is not the same thing as saying that the concepts have no relation to reality. The model of perfect competition is clearly inspired by the wish to examine the properties of an economy with many producers and consumers and the more or less free flow of resources between sectors by the mechanism of exchange. But *model* is the operative word here since a model takes a system of thought and imposes it upon the relations to be studied without justifying the correspondence between the movements and relations within the model to those being examined. It is like argument by analogy which has great expositional qualities but which ultimately breaks down even though the model can always run on.

To bring this section to a close we will summarize its relevance for a history of economic thought. It suggests that each school of economic thought can be probed and dissected to reveal a number of elements. Abstraction utilized within the theory is to be examined and analysed for its causative and empirical content, this last factor including notions drawn from different stages of historical development. The concepts used can be analysed to reveal whether they are consistent historically or otherwise with the real relations under study or whether they are merely imposed upon those relations. These different elements are combined to produce the specific theory concerned. This theory can itself be developed further on its own terms to bring out its essential content. If there are conceptual problems they are not likely to be found in the theory as presented. The result of this may be to produce logical inconsistencies within the theory shown, for example, by the Cambridge critique of neo-classical capital theory, or conceptual inadequacies may be produced as we have illustrated for the Walrasian auctioneer.

These problems within the theories concerned will rarely be due to logical inconsistencies since these are most readily eliminated usually with little or no necessary break in concept. It is much more important to reveal conceptual inadequacies, for these provide the basis for posing new problems which break with the mistakes of the old. Nor should we presume that the deeper the conceptual inadequacies the deeper the theoretical inadequacies since conceptual inconsistency is the product of mixing elements of explanation and may be the richer for it. But the criteria of richness does itself pose the question of assessment from outside the theory under consideration. Here we must confront each school of thought with an explanation of reality that differs from its own. In particular, it will differ through abstraction over what is real and what is appearance. By doing so, it can assess the extent to which the theory being criticized explains reality as well as revealing why the theory should appear to have validity where it does not. In short, whilst an internal examination and critique of a theory may at most be guided by an alternative theory, but according to the propositions already developed in this section, a more complete assessment requires the explicit presence of the critic's views. These need not necessarily be laid out in advance and made explicit but may emerge through the means of the critique. This is the method we will pursue here.

Classical Political Economy

In the next sections, we will attempt to apply the prescriptions of the previous section to the underlying method of various schools of economic thought. Some details of their economic analysis will be discussed in later chapters. We begin with classical political economy and deal with three theorists only – Smith, Ricardo and John Stuart Mill. What these writers share in common is the view that it is important to analyse classes in capitalist society.

To some extent each had the same stereotyped notion of what constituted the typical landlord, capitalist and worker. Landlords consumed rent unproductively through luxury expenditure on items for consumption and to maintain retainers to provide services. Capitalists are the dynamic element in society, receiving the reward of profit for their abstinence which provides for accumulation and growth in the economy. The working class are employed by capital through wage payments and these payments serve to reproduce the labour force. The extent of the working population available to be employed is determined by Malthusian theory. If wages exceed an historically determined subsistence level, then population will expand as more children will be bred and survive. The population will decline if wages fall below the subsistence level. Wages themselves, at least in terms of material goods, are determined by the supply of labour and by the demand which is closely related to the capital advanced as a whole which is divided into wage payments and purchases of physical inputs. Accordingly, the market for labour adjusts like the market for goods by expanding when the wage is higher than an equilibrium subsistence level and declining when it falls below this level, although the mechanism is through reproduction rather than through production.

Classical political economy is also considered to have uniformly accepted Say's Law, the notion that supply creates its own demand, particularly through the influence of Keynes who excepted Malthus from this because of his assigning a demand creating role for landlords out of their expenditure of rent. A more realistic assessment of the relationship between classical political economy and Say's Law is one that sees it as a highly abstract concept for that school. As such, it allows an understanding, whatever its merits, of the processes of production and exchange (in particular for growth, value and distribution). It does so without necessarily denying the possibility of general overproduction or cyclical movements. This remains a secondary or at least a more complex focus for study, one for which the earlier questions are prior. Not surpisingly, the priority given by Keynes to the denial of Say's Law reflects a different ordering of economic relations and one that tends to see classical political economy as necessarily holding fast to the Law.

Whatever the features which in common constitute the school of classical political economy there remain considerable differences between them and we deal with each of those mentioned in turn. Adam Smith is best remembered for his economics through the *The Wealth of Nations*, but he was a scholar who bridged the social sciences, history and philosophy. It is well-recogized that there is a cohesion in the various fields in which he studied. One branch of the Adam Smith 'industry' is therefore to examine the extent to which he is or is not conceptually consistent between his contributions to the various social sciences. We are more concerned with the way in which his 'non-economic' studies informed his understanding of the economy. From his writings on moral philosophy, and in particular from *The Theory of Moral Sentiments*, two underlying human propensities can be seen to have guided Smith's understanding of society. He believes that the contradictory motives of self-interest and fellow-feeling lie behind human behaviour. Moreover, society is formed in a way that unconsciously attempts to reconcile these motives. When one or the other begins to dominate through social relations that co-ordinate the two, then the other operates to amend the social relations to produce a greater harmony and order of the two interests.

Whilst self-interest and fellow-feeling have equal status as underlying human propensities, they do not have equal causative significance. It is the motive of fellow-feeling that tends to produce harmony, and selfishness that makes rules necessary for its achievement through the controls provided by the laws of justice (including property) and morality. These in turn accommodate self-interest through punishment for harming others and by providing esteem in the eyes of society. For Smith, the propensity of self-interest is the stronger of the two since it is dearer to the emotions of the individual concerned. Consequently the individual should moderate his behaviour and the judge should recognize an inability to appreciate the strength of feeling of the judged, but it must be expected that self-interest will prevail. If for the judge we substitute the institutions and relations of society, then we have an idea of the underlying propensities that have to be accommodated and how this might be achieved.

It is not our intention here to explain why Smith should have subscribed to the moral philosophy that he did. Clearly, the emergence of capitalism intensifies the pursuit of self-interest in the sphere of economic relations and makes sharper the problem of explaining, let alone justifying, selfishness against altruism as the support of class divisions by a religious ideology is ended. More important for our purposes is to observe that Smith would necessarily consider that society reaches the end of its path of evolution when it organises a compatibility between the pursuit of self-interest and the common good. Generally the invisible hand operates to co-ordinate the actions of individuals to produce social outcomes that are both unintended and potentially the opposite to their individual basis in self-interest or fellow-feeling. Smith's notion that under capitalism we receive our goods through the self-interest of the producers rather than through their benevolence is always used as the classic reference to illustrate the harmony between self-interest and the social good: 'It is not from the benevolence of the butcher, the brewer, or the baker that we expect our dinner, but from their regard to their own interest', *The Wealth of Nations*, p. 119.

Significantly, he argues in equal measure that benevolence in the market place can produce the opposite effect for society, thereby justifying, indeed demanding, the pursuit of self-interest under capitalism, as long as it does not involve violating the rules of exchange. It is this which explains Smith's opposition to most forms of trade restriction, such as apprenticeships, and all forms of combination whether by producers to raise prices (the more likely case) or workers to raise wages. This attitude is extended to the 'market' that produces labour, namely reproduction, so that Smith opposed a liberal Poor Law as a system of relief that simply perpetuated and flooded the labour market. This reactionary doctrine was also taken up by Ricardo and Malthus and continues today in milder forms as the criticism of social security as the source of 'unemployment'. Paradoxically, for classical political economy, the opposition to the Poor Law could be based on a misplaced sympathy for the labouring class as a whole. The same is rarely true of the exponents of its modern version, although a shared view is the notion of working class propensities in the one case to over-breeding, in the other to laziness.

For Smith then, interventions against exchange and its expansion whether by the state, merchants, in foreign trade or by a landed interest are all equally to be condemned. In short, Smith sees capitalism as the resting place for the evolution of social relations precisely because exchange allows the pursuit of self-interest to be harmoniously compatible with the common good. It is necessary for society to be organized as far as possible to permit the transformation of self-interest into common good through the mechanism of individualized exchange. Thus: 'People of the same trade seldom meet together, even for merriment and diversion, but the conversation ends in a conspiracy against the public, or in some contrivance to raise prices. It is impossible indeed to prevent such meetings, by any law which either could be executed, or would be consistent with liberty and justice. But though the law cannot hinder people of the same trade from sometimes assembling together, it ought to do nothing to facilitate such assemblies, much less to render them necessary.' *The Wealth of Nations*, p. 232.

Smith belonged to the Scottish school of materialist philosophy for whom man's natural propensities are crucial. Of these the desire to satisfy insatiable wants is the basis for a continual change in society and leads to a focus on the means of satisfying wants through productive activity. History is divided by Smith into four stages according to the predominant means of earning a subsistence. These stages are the rude, pastoral, agricultural and commercial. Each contains a structure of economic relations and an associated superstructure. Smith constantly draws comparisons between the different forms of organization of these stages. But he goes beyond this. His understanding of one stage is often imposed upon another so that his analysis of the commercial or capitalist stage is often made as if it were an earlier stage. One major difference in the commercial stage is that it realizes the perfect mechanism for co-ordinating society's division of labour. The supposedly natural propensities to truck, barter and exchange passes through the stage of barter from the stage of trucking to the stage of exchange as society progresses from the rude to the commercial.

Due to the breadth of his knowledge and the wish to compare and contrast different stages of development of society and the forces that give rise to a transition between stages, Smith draws upon a wealth of empirical and (particularly) historical material. This does not serve simply to illustrate his arguments but is also incorporated into his analysis as a means of posing and solving theoretical problems. Here there is a complete contrast with Ricardo. Although Ricardo wishes to apply his analysis to the important policy decisions of the day, concerning taxation and free trade, it is the narrowness of the underlying sources of Ricardo's theory that is crucial.

Ricardo can best be seen as attempting to understand capitalism by the use of a value theory based on labour-time but in which the concept of value is not seen as playing an underlying role within the theory. Value, as determined by labour-time of production, is identified at times with exchange value so that when the two diverge quantitatively, Ricardo's theory is thrown into turmoil. Ricardo's theory then has a beautiful simplicity precisely because of the purity of the abstract concept that he uses and the naivety with which he connects it to more complex concepts, as if or in the hope that they were not more complex. Consequently, it is relatively simple for any historian of economic thought to locate themselves in relation to Ricardo. If a theory based on labour time is deemed to be important, as in Marxist theory, then Ricardo can be assessed for the insights that he produces by utilizing a concept of value based on labour-time and for the confusions that he creates by identifying value with exchange value. Alternatively, for those who reject a value theory based on labour-time, Ricardo is to be praised for his analysis of exchange value since he shows that his labour theory of value is an obstacle to the proper determination of price. In conformity with their own theory, they see Ricardo as attempting to shed the labour theory of value. If he does so, we can observe that he would also shed the insights that his value theory contains by its use of labour as a category underlying the explanation of price and profit.

In his political economy, John Stuart Mill unconsciously begins to reject Ricardo's value theory whilst confessing himself an ardent supporter of it. He intends merely to tie up a few loose ends and to improve the presentation. By doing this and in conjunction with other modifications in his theory, he comes much closer to a way of thinking characteristic of marginalism and for this reason is often considered a bridge between classical political economy and marginalism. Like Smith, and unlike Ricardo, Mill's studies took him into many fields of enquiry. But, in comparison with Smith, Mill's political economy is relatively uninformed by his knowledge from outside the subject. The major exception concerns his analysis of classes. For Mill, the laws of production are natural and quite independent of the social or other economic arrangements that are made to accommodate them. They simply form a relationship between man and the objects of nature which is fixed by what is physically possible between the two. Here we are reminded of the neo-classical theory of production whose production functions are supposed to incorporate what is technically possible in providing outputs from given inputs.

In contrast to production, distribution as the other great department of political economy is taken by Mill to be subject to social laws. Different stages of development of society are characterized by different social relations for the distribution of products. The laws of production are independent of the arrangements for distribution, and the latter alone determines the value of commodities. Distribution is itself composed of two elements, competition and custom, and only the first of these is subject to laws because custom is necessarily less systematic and has the function of protecting the weak (rather than maintaining the strong over the weak!) Consequently, Mill sees class relations in distributional terms and goes on to associate these relations with the three great factors of production: capital, labour and land. This is done not only for capitalism but for all societies and, where factor ownerships coincide, the individual concerned takes on a dual class position. Unfortunately this would imply that the self-employed, land-owning farmer is his own master and slave, capitalist and wage-labourer, and lord and serf. Apart from this unacceptable conclusion, we note that Mill again adopts a position that has an affinity with marginalism: factors of production are seen as the sources of revenue but otherwise are independent of the class relations of production.

Marginalism and Modern Economics

Methodologically, the major characteristic of marginalism and of the schools of thought that comprise much of modern economics besides, is its futile attempt to free itself from the necessity of an abstraction that assigns a different status to different concepts within the theory. Central to this endeavour is the division of the economy from the rest of society so that the economy can be studied in isolation from social relations in general, just as economics becomes a separate discipline from other social sciences, history and philosophy. What modern economics has done is to avoid the question of the relationship between economy and society. It is not an easily answered question. But it is perhaps clear that capital, for example, cannot be adequately understood in the absence of a notion of class relations. It is such an absence which is characteristic of the notion of capital as a stock whether it be of money, physical objects or an acquired skill. Consequently, the main tendency of modern economics is to leave uninvestigated its own method and the historical, empirical and social underpinnings of the subject unchallenged. As a result, economics remains limited to a study of the economy by relationships between concepts which contain very little explanatory power. It is, however, crucial to realize that the attempt to eliminate abstraction is bound to be futile. That it is necessarily present gives rise to debates within modern economics over the abstractions to be used, although this is not usually recognized as such. It is seen rather as a debate over the assumptions to be employed in models and over the causative significance of different variables within the models. We explain this and its consequences in more detail later. First we explain why those, even critical of modern economics, often fail to recognize its abstractions.

Marx characterizes the economics that began to emerge in his time in reaction against Ricardo's value theory as being vulgar. The theory attempts to deny that labour is the sole source of value as this increasingly became a radical notion of the right of labourers to the total product of their work. The vulgarity of the work derives from its preoccupation with appearances and this can be understood in two ways. In terms of the theory itself, no distinction is made between reality and appearance so that the identification of underlying relationships is denied. All that can be studied are the relationships between concepts that have an equal, explanatory status so that no conceptual content can be added by the theory. To use a simple analogy, a study of the relationship between two different measures of weight can add nothing to an understanding of weight itself. Similarly, an economics that is concerned purely with the quantitative relations between outputs, inputs and prices, in which these quantities all have an equal conceptual status, will be unable to explain or examine economic relations in a way that adds to the understanding already contained in the concepts used.

Modern economics may also be considered vulgar for its preoccupation with what are appearances for other theories. For Marx, the vulgar economics of his time fails to try and explain why wages, prices and profits exist in a capitalist society. They are simply taken for granted without revealing any underlying basis for their existence in the capitalist organization of society. The categories of political economy become identified with ahistorical causes that cannot thereby produce explanations that are specific to capitalism. Profit, for example, is the reward for waiting or abstinence.

It is the vulgarity of modern economics, its self-confessed preoccupation with the relationship between what are at once both simple and complex concepts (such as prices) that might lead us to believe that no abstraction is contained within the theory. This is incorrect since the concepts utilized are necessarily divorced from the object of study and never reproduce it in its full complexity.

Despite its vulgarity, modern economics does have an explanatory power and has concepts with different status. The different causative status of concepts can be derived from two sorts of explanations, one that we shall term external and the other internal to the theory.

Let us begin with explanation external to the theory. Because of the division of the economy in the theory from the rest of society, non-economic relations within the theory are taken to be exogenously determined parameters. This becomes true even of what are economic parameters for the theory such as technology, factor endowments and utility. These are taken as given, the assumptions for the model of the theory, with the result that they determine what happens within the theory since this itself contains little causative conceptual content. Economics divides its variables into those that are exogenous and those that are endogenous and the latter are determined by the former. For example, in general equilibrium theory, technology, initial factor endowments and preferences determine equilibrium. They are taken as given along with a set of prices which can be examined for its properties of existence, uniqueness and stability. The significance of the existence of prices remains unexplored, but it can be argued that prices are determined by the exogenously given parameters of the model as if this were an explanation of prices. Paradoxically, all the explanation relies upon factors that are external to the model, which remain unanalysed let alone explained by the theory.

The same is true in the use of partial rather than general equilibrium. For partial equilibrium takes as exogenous parameters, what would be endogenous variables for a general equilibrium. For example, a single market equilibrium takes as given the prices in all other markets including those of substitutes. A change in the price of a substitute can be seen as causing a change in the price of the good with which we are concerned. For a general equilibrium theorist this is a mode of argument which is itself only valid under special assumptions which, if made clear, would prove unacceptable because of the interdependence of all prices and markets. But things are not so simple. Partial equilibrium, by taking as exogenous causative factors that are nevertheless economic, is able to explain aspects of the economy within economic relations. This gives it some conceptual content at the economic level. In contrast, general equilibrium, by perfecting the logic of the economics, removes explanatory power from within the analysis of economic relations and endows it upon what are truly exogenous factors to its economics. A tension exists then between the logic of the analysis and its explanatory power. Nor is this an idle debate. It explains the appeal of partial over general equilibrium analysis, quite apart from the complexity of the latter for which everything depends upon everything else. For without partial equilibrium the specificity of different sorts of revenue becomes lost so that rent, wages and profits are indistinguishable conceptually, apart from differences in the conditions of supply and demand. In principle, however, they are determined in exactly the same way as any other price. A commitment then to partial equilibrium against the logic of general equilibrium is an attempt to maintain a certain causative element within economics that would otherwise be lost. At the turn of the twentieth century a debate within marginalism took place precisely on these grounds as partial equilibrium theorists stood against the sweeping tide of general equilibrium (see chapters 6 and 7).

One property of a causation derived from the relation between exogenous and endogenous variables is that it runs along the lines of mathematical deduction or determination. The parameters of the system are the basis for calculating the outcome for the economy and are also interpreted as forming the cause of that outcome. As we have seen, this is precisely and paradoxically because these parameters themselves remain unexplained. Causation within modern economics does not, however, remain limited to this relationship between the external and internal variables of the system. There is also a possible causation internal to the theory.

We say possible because it may be excluded. For example, in general equilibrium theory, the model determines prices and quantities simultaneously so that none has a greater causal significance than any other and ultimately causation lies with the exogenous parameters. More generally, the simultaneous equations of a model can be assigned a causative significance that endows certain variables with a higher status than others. In interpreting a particular equation, causation can be assumed to run from one side of the equality to the other or vice versa. Alternatively an equation may hold in which the lines of causation cut across the various variables that are taken to be equal. For a system of equations, causation may be interpreted to correspond to the variables that stand on opposite sides of the equalities and to follow the directions taken in solving the system. Alternatively, causation may be simultaneous, that is mutually interdependent, or not follow the structure of causation suggested by the equalities themselves.

The latter is not rare, for the process of exposition of a theory, including its internal causative structure, is liable to lead to a construction of the model's equations in conformity with the causal structure for the purposes of clarity. For example, the Keynesian consumption function $C = cY$ would explain consumption as being determined by the level of income. On the other hand, endogenous and exogenous variables can be mixed up within a model. In principle, a reduced form for econometric estimation (or for making clear the source of external causation) can be calculated. For example, the equality between the supply of and demand for money written in the form $M_S = M_D (r, p, Y)$ where M_S, M_D, r, p and Y are the supply and demand for money, the rate of interest, price level, and level of income respectively is open to a variety of causal interpretations that do not necessarily correspond to the demand for money as a whole moving into equality with the supply or vice versa. The speculative element alone could be taken to be causal in bringing the equality about so that the transactions and precautionary motives would be as passive as the assumed exogenous supply of money, except in so far as other causes bring changes in the variables upon which these motives for holding money depend.

More generally, it is well-recognized that modern economic models contain determination by the relationship between exogenous and endogenous variables but also in terms of underlying structural relations which are usually captured in the form of one set of equations rather than another. Whilst two sets of equations may be equivalent in determining endogenous by exogenous variables they will incorporate a differing causative content internal to the theory. How is this possible?

First, the causative content does not come from the equations themselves. For internal as for external causation, the equations themselves do not contain within them the principles of causation adopted. The equations are neutral in relation to causation, since they are consistent with any structure of causative direction. The principles of causation within the theory then are external to the equations of the models and we must ask from where the causative structure comes. This is an important and puzzling question since we have already argued that modern economics has a tendency to do away with abstraction and treat all concepts as having an equal and unexplained status. Yet for one set of concepts within the theory to have a greater causal role than others is to place them at a higher level of abstraction and utilize them as underlying forces. For example, in Keynesian theory, the determining role is played by effective demand in bringing aggregate supply and demand into equality. Consequently, supply is understood only on the basis of the demand which creates it, whereas demand itself can be formed independently of supply.

The source of causation within modern economics is to be found in a conceptual inconsistency which explains why the tendency to eliminate abstraction within the theory can coexist with an internal causative structure. Modern economics is rooted in an analysis of the appearances generated by capitalist exchange relations. These relations are the means by which production is organized socially, although they are distinct from the production process itself. They represent the fact that economic relations are socialized in a particular way and these socialized relations should be the starting point for an analysis of the economy. Exchanges themselves, however, only take place between individuals and so, in principle, each act of exchange is unique. It is defined by the commodities exchanged, the individuals concerned, the time and place, the extent of credit etc. If a theory is not to pursue the fatuous task of providing a mirror image of every exchange that takes place, certain uniformities must be assumed to exist that delineate between some exchanges but which render others homogeneous. Within modern economics these simplifying assumptions are drawn from exchange itself and do reflect certain tendencies within the capitalist economy. A uniform price for a commodity is generally assumed and justified on the basis that competition tends to create uniform prices. Similar assumptions are generally made about wages and profits.

These assumptions do correspond to real tendencies within the capitalist economy and are modern economics' way of recognizing that there are socialized economic relations that form the underlying context in which individual economic activity takes place. However, because modern economics bases itself on the aggregated atomized behaviour of individuals, it creates a conceptual inconsistency by its simultaneous employment of social categories, such as uniform prices. If the economy is made up of the co-ordinated acts of individuals through exchange then each act of exchange is individual and should be treated as such. Otherwise the assumptions underlying the uniformity of various exchange relations will prove to be inconsistent with their actual heterogeneity. This theoretical problem is recognized within modern economics by one response, which is to make finer and finer divisions within the theory, to disaggregate sector by sector. But some uniformity always remains to plague the individualistic basis of the theory. To displace one model by another which is more general and renders the other a special case is to recognize the problem but not to solve it. This can only be done by a method of abstraction that awards a different status to the concepts within the theory and sees the more complex concepts as the reproduction of the simpler underlying ones. This is precisely the method that modern economics rejects by drawing its concepts from the appearances of individual acts co-ordinated through exchange.

The inconsistent conflation of concepts at a social and individual level then is the result of a denial of levels of abstraction within the theory. It is also an index of the inability to realize this denial absolutely. It has the effect of introducing a causative structure into the theory. When a social category is assumed to exist independently of the aggregated individual actions upon which it is based, then that social category determines that the individual actions should be consistent with it rather than vice versa. Differences between schools of modern economics are the result of differences in the causative structures utilized which in turn reflect different forms in which social and individual categories are inconsistently combined.

A summary will be in order here by way of a comparison with Dobb (1972). The role and nature of causation external to the theory is relatively clear. By mathematical methods or otherwise, endogenous variables are calculated and hence considered determined by the exogenous. This is well discussed by Dobb in his introductory chapter. He argues, as we have done, that explanation then lies outside the theory. Dobb also recognizes that equations as such are not the source of a causative content but are more by nature a basis for tautology. The more equations alone fill out the theory, the less the explanatory content. Here, however, we begin to diverge from Dobb by our identifying an internal causative content. The source of this is the conflation of an individualized with a socialized concept of the economy. But the content is not independent of the mathematical structure given to the models thereby constructed. The mathematics is both the mechanism and the form in which the internal causation is incorporated into the theory. Who, for example, would argue that the Keynesian neo-classical synthesis is independent of the structure of causation intrinsic to equations given by the IS/LM curves?

In contrast to our position, Dobb carries over the neutrality of the mathematics for external causation to causation internal to the theory. The basis for doing so is that the source of the causation lies elsewhere, which we accept, but this does not render the mathematics neutral nor independent of the causative content unless it is purely based on external factors. For Dobb: 'All that can be shortly said, I think, about such an allegedly "neutral" corpus is that when carefully formulated and analysed it will be found to be extremely thin in factual content: i.e. its apparent neutrality is because it contains very little in the way of factual statement about economic situations or processes and their behaviour – so little, perhaps, as to evoke serious doubt as to whether it is entitled to rank as an economic theory at all in the sense of a theory that *explains* social action and behaviour.' p. 11.

We disagree. It is important to recognize the factual content of the theory and that it does explain social action and behaviour. Only by doing so can we assess its validity critically.

Our remarks can be illustrated by considering various schools of modern economics. Neo-classical general equilibrium theory, for example, presumes that competition establishes uniform prices by the actions of individuals whereas it could be equally argued that competition would create many different prices between individuals. Because prices are taken to be uniform, the conditions for the existence, stability and uniqueness of equilibrium can be examined as if competition would cause equilibrium to be attained when these conditions are satisfied. Competition within the theory makes individuals act in a uniform way and makes equilibrium possible, whereas competition concerns individual attempts to act differently for which equilibrium would be impossible. To some extent these problems have been broached within modern economics either by a game-theoretic approach to individual economic agents, for which an equilibrium probabilistic distribution of behaviour emerges, or by the introduction of monopolistic or imperfect competition. Taken to their logical conclusions these theories would treat each individual exchange as distinct and lose any causative content that they contain.

Neo-classical general equilibrium theory is based on the view that the market works well to co-ordinate individual economic behaviour. Macroeconomics is concerned to reassess that conclusion by giving certain aggregate categories priority over others in determining the context in which individual economic behaviour takes place. Keynesian economics, for example, in its traditional form gives causal priority to the determinants of aggregate effective demand. But because the ineffectuality of demand is felt through the market by the exchange activities of individuals, for conceptual consistency, the level of effective demand should be determined by individual acts of exchange. Again, this problem has been accommodated, by the evolution (through the reappraisal of Keynes' literature) of disequilibrium macro-economics. What the theory gains in consistency is matched by its loss in causative explanation as macro-economics becomes a more sophisticated version of micro-economic general equilibrium theory. For the Keynesian theory associated with Kaldor, Pasinetti and Kalecki, the level of aggregate demand is calculated along the lines of expenditures out of profits and wages rather than from the macro-economic aggregates of national income accounting. Just as the use of these particular aggregates gives the theory its causative content so they are themselves inconsistent with their exchange based origins in individual transactions. Capitalists earn what they spend as a class, if not as individuals, but what they spend as individuals is the sum of their individual expenditures.

For the Sraffian system of thought, the conflation of individual and social categories takes place through the assumption of uniform levels of prices and most importantly through uniform rates of profits and wages. Such assumptions are justified in terms of competition in exchange, a reliance upon the outcome of transactions between individuals. The resultant inverse relation between the uniform rates of wages and profits creates the impression that the economy is determined by a distributional struggle between classes, although this struggle is itself introduced exogenously. In fact, because competition exists between individual capitalists and workers, the distributional struggle should be located in terms of individual acts of exchange producing a variety of wage and profit rates. Consequently, the inconsistency produced by combining the social categories of uniform wages and profits with their individual determination through competition, creates a causal relation from wages, profits and technology to prices. Elsewhere, (Fine (1980)) we have criticized this theory for its understanding of production, distribution and exchange (see chapter 8 in the context of theories of the falling rate of profit).

We have offered quite a lengthy exposition of the way in which abstraction is incorporated into modern economics to give a causative structure.

Earlier, we argued that abstraction also involves the incorporation of an empirical element. Modern economics is predominantly based upon a methodology of positivism for which the real world can be represented by facts which are external to the theory and against which the theory can be tested for validity (in the negative sense of not being rejected). In addition, because verification of the theory becomes focused on the criteria of compatibility with external facts, the validity of the theory comes to rest exclusively upon this rather than by examination of its internal conceptual consistency and method.

In this manner, facts, which *contra* positivism can only be interpreted and used within a theoretical framework, enter merely for the purposes of verification and so give the theory little empirical content. The theory is divorced from the historical and social significance of the empirical material it is attempting to explain.

Nevertheless, empirical material does enter the theory in the form of the assumptions of the model. Modern economists often discuss the 'realism' of their assumptions by which they mean a correspondence with supposedly externally given facts. A debate has taken place between Friedman and Samuelson over whether assumptions should be realistic or not. For Friedman, the realism of an assumption is irrelevant to the theory's verifiability and the more unreal and simplistic are the assumptions, the more a theory potentially has in explanatory power. Here Friedman is searching for a depth of causal explanation by a leap from abstract, simple concepts to complex ones, given externally in the form of facts. For Samuelson, assumptions must also be realistic. They form after all the most simple deductions of the theory. Samuelson pursues conceptual consistency at the expense of reducing causality, with concepts all being reduced towards the same level of complexity. In either case, the method of incorporating empirical material into the theory creates a distorted connection and dichotomy between the simple concepts or assumptions which are more or less unreal and the facts which are complex and real.

Apart from the method of incorporating empirical material, there is the social and historical origins of the material incorporated. Because modern economics bases itself predominantly upon exchange relations as relations between individuals, the capitalist economy is treated as if it were a mode of production composed of independent commodity producers freely enjoined in acts of exchange. At the same time, the realities of contemporary capitalism make it almost impossible to ignore the existence of categories specific to it such as wages and profits. Because these cannot be explained by exchange as such, a dependence is made upon ahistorical conditions, ones which would apply in every society such as technology, labour, utility, a stock of means of production, and so on. In this way, the major classes of capitalism are first identified through exchange by the revenues that they receive. This identification may rest there, and the role of classes be analysed by their role in exchange, or it may be carried further to associate particular classes with particular historical conditions. Thus, Sraffian theory identifies capital with profits to be earned according to capital advanced and labour with wages according to labour advanced. These classes meet in exchange and conduct a distributional struggle over their respective revenues as if they were two independent producers each monopolizing a means of production that is essential to the other. The Kaldor/Kalecki version of classes treats them according to the expenditures that they make. Neo-classical theory identifies classes according to the factors that they supply but then abandons exchange as a basis for explaining classes and relies upon ahistorical causes. Profit arises from abstinence and the productivity of time embodied in capital stock, wages from the disutility of work and the utility of leisure and rent from the fixedness of land in supply. We take this up in more detail in chapter 6.

Marxist and Radical Political Economy

Over the past fifteen years or so, there has been a resurgence of interest in Marxist political economy and, associated with it, radical economics. To some extent, and certainly for many involved, the distinction is forced and arbitrary. The stimulus to both has been the rise of a radical student movement, the stumbling and falling of the world capitalist economy, and the inability of orthodox economics to respond to either of these factors whether theoretically or empirically. Every direction in which the student or enquiring mind turns suggests that the harmony or even Keynesian disharmony of exchange relations is an inadequate basis for understanding capitalist society. Crisis, power and inequality are the concepts which seem more appropriate.

This is certainly the thrust of radical economics. As a result, it has been able to produce analyses in areas such as imperialism, sexism, unemployment, distribution, power and alienation, urban crisis, welfare provision, militarism, and technology and so on. An examination of empirical material in the light of these concepts strongly suggests a ready correspondence to reality in contrast to the narrow confines imposed by the method and subject matter of orthodox economics. Usually, but not always, the core of this correspondence is to be located in the class content of the analysis. This is the starting point for radical economics and characterizes it and distinguishes it from the orthodoxy. But is this enough? Class as a vantage point does not constitute a theory, it is merely one element within it. It is here that radical economics has a weakness. Implicitly it is often presumed that a class analysis or its associated instrument, such as exploitation or imperialism, is a sufficient basis on which to go out and order the world as it is presented to us empirically. Where the radical theory is more developed it is often done so carelessly without due attention to its consistency with the perceived underlying role assigned to class relations.

It is these considerations which have led us to criticize Sraffian economics and also class-based Keynesian theories. It is not the presence of class as such, which is to be deplored but the way in which it is incorporatd. For some, adopting such a critical stance, the result is to emphasize what are the 'bourgeois' elements of the theory and thereby to dismiss it. Certainly these elements should be brought to the fore and even emphasized since their mode of presentation is incomprehensible without the element of class relations with which they are combined. Both to understand the specific theory concerned and the aspect of class relations that they capture, due attention must be given to the theory as a whole. This is even more so for less pure subjects of economic theory. Consequently, criticism is not dismissal but an attempt to comprehend, extract and transform the positive elements of a theory under assessment. In attempting to convince others to abandon a theory or one or more of its elements, it may be better to be more diplomatic than critical. This is another question and is one on which radical economics has an excellent record.

To some extent it has done so by maintaining a distance from Marxist political economy. This is identified with a preoccupation with Marx's own theoretical contribution, one which is seen as confined to overly abstract questions and of little relevance to the immediacy of late twentieth century capitalism's problems. For many, the dogma of Paul Samuelson is not to be rejected only to be replaced by that of Karl Marx. This is a legitimate attitude but it does not excuse the failure to examine the theoretical content of either writer, and of others. Such an examination is undertaken in this book and it is one which is predominantly informed by Marx's theoretical insights. But the result is not to substitute a Marxist standard by which to judge economic theory for the retrospect of neo-classical economics. We do not ask to what extent do the various theories considered match up to and correspond to Marxism. By examining different aspects and problems of the theories we hope to demonstrate, not to assert, the legitimacy of the approach which informs our analysis. Neutrality is impossible but the alternative is not necessarily dogma.

Further Reading

There is an enormous volume of literature on method, supporting and criticizing almost as many different positions and taking off in all sorts of directions. A starting point could be Mohun's essay in Green and Nore (1980), Chapter 1 of Fine (1980), and Green in Green and Nore (1977). Skinner gives an excellent introduction to Adam Smith's *The Wealth of Nations* in the Pelican Edition by exploring the evolution of Smith's economics from his moral and materialist philosophy. We would, however, treat with hesitation his notion of equilibrium in Smith despite the use of a natural price (see chapter 5). Harris (1981) in chapter 6, gives an account of Say's Law for classical political economy and Hollander (1980) examines the significance (or otherwise) of Ricardian economics for the socialist notion of natural right to labour. Dobb (1973) in his opening chapter has a discussion of causation and explanation in economic theory. The best introduction to radical economics is to be found in various URPE (Union of Radical Political Economy) publications. The equivalent to this American body in Britain, CSE (Conference of Socialist Economists), is more based upon Marxist political economy. We particularly recommend Edwards et al. (1972) and Elson (1979) as representative samples respectively.

2
Smith and Marx on the Division of Labour

On the Division of Labour

The division of labour in most societies, and particularly in modern capitalism, is extremely complex. Who does what job, in what way and why? The question can be approached in as many ways as there are divisions of labour and these are numerous quite apart from the different products created. Division of labour can be analysed on the basis of male and female, intellectual and manual, across countries as foreign trade, skilled and unskilled, productive and unproductive (in whatever way this is interpreted), manual and white collar, managers and managed, services and manufactures, and so the list could run on. Modern economic analysis has tended to neglect the division of labour as a product of economic and social relations by explaining it in terms of the allocation of each individual to particular jobs according to individual preference and skill (or according to a skill acquired through investment in 'human capital'). What makes the jobs what they are tends to be ignored and subsumed under technology which is assumed to evolve exogenously as technical progress. Economics has become oblivious to the fate of the workers in the jobs that they undertake and the division of labour is taken for granted as a desirable source of increased productivity and growth.

Smith and Marx approach the division of labour openly and directly, being concerned with its relationship to exchange and to the origins and development of capitalism. Here we will attempt to compare and contrast their theories with these aspects in mind and only introduce other aspects of the division of labour to illustrate the nature of their arguments.

Smith on the Division of Labour

Although Smith's *The Wealth of Nations* is best remembered for its theory of *laissez-faire* policy associated with the efficacy of the invisible hand, the importance of the division of labour in this work has also been well-recognized. Indeed, the book opens with a discussion of this topic in its first three chapters and the division of labour is returned to frequently during the course of the analysis both to analyse the effects as well as the causes of its development. For this reason, it is important always to bear in mind the significance of the division of labour for Smith. Even where it is not introduced explicitly in the discussion of some topic, it must be remembered that Smith himself has it in mind. For example, accumulation and price formation are intimately bound to the developing division of labour as we shall argue in chapter 5.

These are two crucial elements in Smith's discussion. He begins by emphasizing that an increasing division of labour is the source of productivity increase. *The Wealth of Nations* opens: 'The greatest improvement in the productive powers of labour and the greater part of the skill, dexterity and judgement with which it is anywhere directed, or applied, seem to have been the effects of the division of labour.' He goes on in the same page to illustrate his view by the division of tasks in pin manufacture, an example that has subsequently become a cliché in the history of economic thought: 'To take an example, therefore, from a very trifling manufacture; but one in which the labour has been very often taken notice of, the trade of the pin-maker.' He suggests that this increased productivity is itself the result of three processes: an increased dexterity that accompanies the confinement of a worker to a specialized task, a saving of the time for the worker from passing from one tool to another (although the product itself may have to pass from hand to hand), and the potential for the invention and introduction of machinery that the division of labour induces. For those looking back upon Smith's theory from the vantage point of neoclassical economics, this analysis could be seen as the counterpart to a consideration of the development of techniques of production and consequently be concerned with the theory of supply. For a Marxist economist, Smith might be seen as being preoccupied with production as a labour process rather than as a neutrally conceived technical relation between men and things.

The second major element in Smith's theory is the notion that the division of labour is provided for and limited by the extent of the market, by demand: 'As it is the power of exchanging that gives occasion to the division of labour, so the extent of this division must always be limited by the extent of that power, or, in other words, by the extent of the market.' (Opening to chapter III). The division of labour increases productivity only at the expense of increasing output and this output must be sold. The argument is made in the context of a single market, mass production of a particular commodity would be unsuitable if its sale were limited to a local market, for example. This conclusion is then applied to the economy as a whole although this is not valid as it stands. For logically it is possible for different sectors of the economy to expand together as they provide markets for each other even if the expansion of a single sector is limited by demand if other sectors do not expand in unison.

For a neo-classical economist, Smith's analysis of the significance of the extent of the market could be seen as a consideration of demand. This complements the theory of supply as the basis for an equilibrium between supply and demand to form prices and outputs. An alternative interpretation is to take one of the aspects of division of labour as determining the other. If productivity increase does not lead to difficulties of sale, then appropriate incomes will be generated to fuel a continuing expansion of output. By contrast, ineffective demand will constrain an increasing output and the associated division of labour.

We accept neither of these interpretations of the manner in which Smith links the productivity increase associated with the division of labour with the limitations placed upon it by the extent of the market. Smith does see these two aspects interacting to produce incomes, prices and expansion but in a way that locates them as underlying forces. The resultant of these forces can only be determined in the context of the wider social considerations in which they are situated. Consequently, it would be erroneous to search in Smith for theoretical evidence supporting the view that supply or demand or their simultaneous interaction is determinant. Certainly such evidence can be found in the form of his presentation of factors that extend the market or those that translate productivity increase into (income and) expenditure increase. However, Smith analysed these factors in a historical and social as well as an economic-theoretic context. The development of transport widens the market by extending existing markets and by creating new ones. The establishment of a socially recognized money improves the efficiency of exchange and through banking mobilizes otherwise idle money for expenditure. In foreign trade and the relations between town and country, particular interest groups can obstruct the development of the division of labour and the extent of the market. Unproductive expenditure by the state or through luxury consumption can have the same effect. These influences are the subject of separate study at various points and in the various different five parts of *The Wealth of Nations*. Their presence and treatment demonstrate Smith's preoccupation with the division of labour and the social as well as the economic factors that influence its progress.

To summarize, Smith locates the wealth of nations in the interaction between a growing division of labour and the extent of market relations. This interaction is not purely economic but is resolved in definite and evolving social relations. Accordingly, Smith's analysis is quite complex combining theoretical and historical argument in confronting the relations between economy and society. However, even though we have suggested that Smith does not determine the economy by economic relations alone, it is clear that the extent of the market and the division of labour do not have equal status within his theory even if each is linked to the other through social relations. The extent of the market takes pride of place over the division of labour. This conclusion can be drawn from the results of Smith's analysis. His overwhelming preference for free trade and lack of state intervention demonstrates a strong tendency to view the expansion of exchange as the driving force of capitalism. His conclusion that the movement of the economy will lead to a stationary state, as accumulation mops up available markets and hence investment opportunities, reveals a priority granted ultimately to the confining extent of the market. (We take this up again in chapter 8.)

Smith's preference for the priority of the extent of the market over the division of labour can also be seen in terms of his approach to the causes, effects and origins of the division of labour. To begin with the last, Smith derives the existence of the division of labour from the supposedly natural propensity of humans to truck, barter and exchange, this itself possibly derived from a more fundamental propensity to exercise persuasion through speech (see the second chapter of the *The Wealth of Nations*). Because Smith derives the division of labour from a natural propensity, the division like the propensity is to be found in all stages of society even if it can only be given full expression in the commercial stage. Accordingly, Smith is able to examine the specifically capitalist division of labour as if it belonged to an earlier stage of society. At times, he argues that the rude society admits no division of labour since each hunter can produce goods as they are individually required. On the other hand, randomly distributed skills will be utilized even in the rude society to form certain specializations. However, whilst these differences in talent are the origin of the division of labour, the differences are themselves many times magnified by the assignation of workers to particular tasks in the division of labour created by commercial society.

In addition, Smith's ahistorical approach to the division of labour is exemplified by his analysis of the preconditions for its existence and extension and its relation to stock and accumulation. This is in part his focus in Book II of *The Wealth of Nations*. A division of labour requires a stock of raw materials and subsistence goods so that production can be undertaken without the necessity of the self-manufacture of these being imposed on each producer. Smith in fact makes this argument in the context of an independent producer for which the division of labour cannot be extended too far since only one person is employed! He goes on to argue that accumulation is required to extend the stock so that workers' subsistence as well as raw materials can be expanded but this involves a leap from the petty commodity producer to the capitalist mode of production in which wage-labour is employed. Smith, however, is only concerned with the use value requirements for the extended division of labour, that more means of subsistence and more means of production must be available. By focusing on these requirements the changing relations of production, from petty to capitalist commodity production, pass unobserved. It is as if the accumulation of a stock is by itself sufficient to generate an increased division of labour including the associated wage relations.

But this is not quite fair, since Smith sees as necessary another condition: that there be sufficient demand for the expanded output and the source of increased demand is to be provided by exchange rather than by truck or by barter. It is this that permits us to conclude that it is the extent of the market that is the driving force of capitalism for Smith. Indeed, it is the development of exchange within the stage of agriculture that is the basis for the development of the commercial stage or capitalism in Smith's theory.

This is most clear in his analysis of the relationship between town and country (see Book III). For Smith, the natural order of progression is from an expansion within the country as a precondition for the development of the town for which means of subsistence and production are provided. The next stage is for capital to be oriented towards the foreign sector. The United States of America is taken as an ideal example. Europe is seen as confirming the theory by the failure of its agriculture to develop sufficiently fast. Commercial policies in favour of the towns and the unproductive maintenance of retainers by the landlord class inhibited but did not prevent the development of capitalism. Instead the development of commerce within the towns places pressure on the country through trade and ultimately triggers the processes in agriculture that have previously been hindered. Commerce can then develop in unison between town and country to their mutual advantage both for gains from trade and from division of labour through extended markets.

Smith's emphasis is on the forces which develop exchange relations. This is exemplified by his focus on the progressive role played by city merchants who buy land. The same applies to the farmers who gain greater independence from landlords in return for a larger surplus which is to be traded by the latter with the town for manufactures. In each case, the merchant and farmer become capitalists by trading more and it is presumed that the supply of wage labour is available for them to do so. In this sense, Smith's preference for the extent of the market over the division of labour reflects a preference for analysing exchange relations over relations of production. How a class of wage labourers is created, rather than provided for, is neglected and the same applies to how this class might react against the division of labour in production that the extending market demands. This is despite Smith's recognition that the developing division of labour strips the worker of skills and renders the labour process tediously repetitive.

Thus, although Smith's analysis starts out with the division of labour in the manufacture of pins, with labourers under the control of a single producer, his main concern is with the division of labour between producers as the sellers of commodities and it is this which gives the extent of the market its predominance in his thought. One of Marx's major criticisms of Smith's analysis of the division of labour is in the latter's failure to emphasize the importance of the distinction between what Marx called for capitalism, the social division of labour and the division of labour within a production process. By the social division of labour Marx meant the division associated with the exchange relations between commodities, each commodity itself being the product of a labour process with a division of labour which is not connected by exchange relations. Smith is certainly aware of the distinction, it is not conceptually difficult. But its significance is lost on him since he simply lumps the two divisions together to form an aggregate division of labour as the basis for assessing productivity potential. Smith is to be congratulated for combining many elements in his theory of the division of labour. Its division by exchange and by the production process is recognized but the emphasis is placed upon the former. This itself leads to a neglect of the role played by the formation of a class of wage labourers in the development of the division of labour and its continuing influence once formed. For Smith these questions are very much reduced to the exchange based formation of an adequate stock of means of production and subsistence.

This is not surprising since for Smith the division of labour is ahistorically conceived both in its origins in natural propensities and in the preconditions for its development in the accumulation of a stock of means of subsistence and production. What Smith believes in addition is that the most efficient means for expanding this aggregate division of labour and rendering it most useful to society is through the mechanism of exchange rather than through truck or barter. So, for him, the division of labour can only become complete in the commercial stage of development. In contrast, for Marx, the division of labour was continuously being transformed rather than completed or perfected in the movement to a stationary state. It is to his analysis that we now turn.

Marx on the Division of Labour

Marx's theory of the division of labour for capitalism takes as crucial the distinction between its social division by commodity exchange and its division within the labour process for which exchange does not intervene directly. Here he criticizes Smith:

Now it is quite possible to imagine, with Adam Smith that the difference between the above social division of labour, and the division in manufacture, is merely subjective, exists merely for the observer who in the case of manufacture can see at a glance all the numerous operations being performed on one spot, while . . . the spreading-out of the work over great areas and the great number of people employed in each branch of labour obscure the connection. But what is it that forms the bond between the independent labours of the cattle-breeder, the tanner and the shoe-maker? It is the fact that their respective products are commodities. What, on the other hand, characterizes the division of labour in manufacture? The fact that the specialized worker produces no commodities.

But in spite of the numerous analogies and links connecting them, the division of labour in the interior of a society, and that in the interior of a workshop, differ not only in degree, but also in kind. *Capital I* pp. 474–5.

Like Smith he recognizes the existence of a division of labour prior to capitalism, but he does not see this simply as an underdeveloped division due to the absence of exchange relations. For Marx, the division of labour is always intimately related to the social relations of production that predominate and is not merely a reflection of the means of truck, barter or exchange (see, for example, comments in the first three chapters of *Capital I*). For capitalism, Marx identifies two tendencies in the so-formed aggregate division of labour which develop with capitalist manufacture and mutually condition each other. One gathers together what were previously independent handicrafts under a single production process thereby developing the division of labour at the level of production at the expense of its social division. The other involves the division of labour within an existing labour process, very much like Adam Smith's pin factory. It may lead through specialization to a development of the social division of labour at the expense of the division of labour in production as what were previously intermediate products in a labour process become independent commodities. For Marx, capitalism tends to expand the realm of commodity production so that the two tendencies, which repeatedly redraw the lines between the division of labour between commodities and within individual production processes, are compatible with an expanding division for each (see Chapter 14 of *Capital I* for this and much of what follows).

The significance of the two forms of the division of labour lies in the difference in the economic relations that each involves. The social division of labour is one between capitalists in competition as individual independent producers. The division of labour within the production process is a relationship between capital and labour and its development is given prior consideration by Marx for its causes and effects as well as for its origins. The confusion between the two divisions of labour and the corresponding relations between capitals as opposed to between capital and labour is polemically illustrated by Marx in terms of the control of production. For whilst the organized division of labour within production is acceptable to the capitalists in their individual factories, the social organization of the division of labour as a whole is totally unacceptable. There the preference is for the more or less free play of market forces that are essential for the existence of capitalist commodity production:

Division of labour within the workshop implies the undisputed authority of the capitalist over men, who are merely the members of a total mechanism which belongs to him. The division of labour within society brings into contact independent producers of commodities, who acknowledge no authority other than that of competition . . . The same bourgeois consciousness which celebrates the division of labour in the workshop . . . as an organization of labour that increases its productive power, denounces with equal vigour every conscious attempt to control and regulate the process of production socially, as an inroad upon such sacred things as the rights of property, freedom and the self-determining 'genius' of the individual capitalist. It is very characteristic that the enthusiastic apologists of the factory system have nothing more damning to urge against a general organization of labour in society than that it would turn the whole of society into a factory (p. 477).

Having established the two forms of the division of labour, Marx can analyse the one within production as a relationship between capital and labour, as the production of value and surplus value. His prime concern in considering capitalist manufacture is to identify how it leads to the production of more surplus value through productivity increases which reduce the value of labour-power. Here Marx emphasizes that the division of labour creates detailed skills and a co-operation between labourers which raises productive power. Two forms of manufacture are identified. Heterogeneous manufacture finds a number of parts independently worked up and then brought together for assembly. Serial manufacture involves the working up of a product piece by piece and corresponds to the modern assembly line although this can combine both forms of manufacturing.

The effect of this division of labour on the working class is to create a hierarchy of skills and wages in correspondence to the increasingly specialized tasks that are undertaken. In many instances, however, the detailed labour becomes increasingly simple even if a certain dexterity is gained with practice. Accordingly, hand in hand with the creation of skilled specialized labour, there is formed an overwhelming amount of simple, unskilled jobs to which a large section of the working class is assigned. Changes are also forced upon the capitalist. Production must be planned and as productivity increase reduces the values of commodities in society these new standards of value must be attained at pain of elimination through competition. This requires certain proportions to be established in the production process. First there is the proportion between the different types of labour in conformity with its division. To employ, in part, a labourer who has learnt a skill in one detailed task, to undertake a task in which he has not the skill is to waste his labour. Second, there is the proportionate division between the 'labour' of superintendence and that of actual production. Finally, there are the proportions between the various physical inputs in the production process to be established.

Each of these proportions requires particular ratios between the quantities involved but these can only be efficiently arranged as the size of capital to purchase these quantities increases. To limit each labourer to a special task, including superintendence, many labourers are required. Many labourers working with increasing productivity need a growing supply of raw materials. The development of the division of labour in production is based upon an accumulation of capital and its control by a single capitalist enterprise. This is a proposition similar to Smith's, that the accumulation of a stock within any society is the precondition for a division of labour to provide for subsistence and physical means of production. In fact, Marx's proposition is a point of departure from Smith's in a number of ways.

He notes first that the accumulation of a stock is the precondition of any production other than the most simple and is not specifically related to a developing division of labour. Where it does induce an increased division of labour, how it does so is extremely important. Within capitalism, it develops in part within production and this demands of the individual capitalist an increase in the size of capital advanced. Consequently, competition, as a result of the social division of labour, coerces individual capitals to accumulate to maintain levels of productivity in conformity with socially necessary labour-time of production. The stock for accumulation is made available by the concentration of ownership of capital. Whilst this might come through the reinvestment of profits, what Marx termed concentration, it might also be brought about through the merging of capitals, a process Marx termed centralization. To begin with then, Marx can be contrasted with Smith for his emphasis on the compulsion to accumulate as the source of a growing division of labour rather than his seeing limits imposed by the extent of the market. Smith also neglects the division of labour that can be promoted by centralization rather than by concentration.

Further, in Smith's neglect of the division of labour within production, the stock required to promote the division of labour in aggregate is almost seen to be accumulated physically by individual capitalists concerned to advance wage goods to labour and to supply raw materials for their use. Society requires such an accumulation, but individual capitalists achieve this effect for themselves through the accumulation of capital as money which can be advanced as wages or to purchase raw materials for immediate use. In failing to recognize this, Smith neglects the markets that are created by capitalists for each other, either directly in the demand for means of production (and their own consumption out of profits), or indirectly through the expenditure of wage revenue on consumption goods. No wonder that Smith focused on the limits imposed by the extent of the market. For he failed to appreciate fully how the creation of wage labour, the most important condition for the development of the division of labour, creates a new market for wage goods. This is despite his observation that the English day-labourer enjoys a higher standard of living than an Indian prince because his wage commands through commodities purchased the labour of many highly productive workers.

Although Smith may have neglected the division of labour in production, Marx does not neglect it in exchange. Nor does he believe that, whilst accumulation can provide a sufficient market for continuing expansion, that it would necessarily continue to do so. As we have observed earlier, Marx recognized that there are two tendencies related to the evolving division of labour, one in exchange and one in production. Their resolution cannot be anticipated since the division of labour is continually subject to transformation. It is not evolving towards a perfection at the pace that the market extends to rest finally in a stationary state, as for Smith. For Marx, the division of labour develops systematically only according to the two tendencies observed and as such is not under the control of the individual capitalists who implement it. The developing division of labour is co-ordinated through exchange relations and based upon production relations. But just as the social division of labour cannot guarantee the production and sale of commodities in the appropriate proportions, so the division of labour within the factory cannot be predetermined because of worker resistance and the responses by individual capitalists to the external pressures of competition.

Both Smith and Marx share the view that the division of labour prepares the way for the introduction of machinery. (For Marx's analysis of the development of machinery production, see chapter 15 of *Capital I*.) For Smith it is simply one factor in explaining productivity increase along with increasing dexterity and the time saved in the worker's no longer passing from one tool to another. For Marx, writing almost a hundred years later, machinery took on a much greater significance. He distinguished production by machinery from production by manufacture. Whereas manufacture adopted existing methods of production and transformed them through the utilization of the co-operation and division of labour, machinery transformed the role played by labour as a whole in the production process. In manufacture, the division of labour brings a range of specialist tools for the workman to use in his detailed task. Machinery production brings the displacement of the worker from the handling of his own tools and instead he becomes a tool of the machine. He becomes robbed even of the simple and specialized task that had been left by manufacture. The pace of work is dictated by the pace of the machine. In short, machinery seizes the division of labour created by manufacture, intensifies it and transforms it into a division of tasks between the parts of the machine to which the labourer becomes an appendage. Not only is labour subordinated to capital economically, it also becomes so technically in the work process.

The significance that Marx gives to machinery is not limited to its effects on the production process and the labourer. For Marx, the development of machinery heralded a new stage in the development of capitalism as a whole, producing transformations in the economy as well as in society. We have seen already that manufacture coerced individual capitalists to accumulate. This coercion intensifies with the introduction of machinery and demands even larger capital outlays, ones which are beyond the power of accumulation through concentration. Centralization, or the reorganization of capital through acquisition, bankruptcy or merger become the order of the day and a credit system through banking must be formed as the means of such an accumulation. The greatest stimulus to production by large-scale machinery can, however, only be realized by reducing or eliminating the potential for competition from capitals which continue to produce by backward methods but remain profitable through imposing long working hours and low wages. Consequently the passing of welfare and labour legislation on behalf of the working class is required for the stage of machine production to become fully established and dominant over other forms of capitalist production. This is discussed in Fine and Harris (1979). This stage has, however, been more focused upon and termed as the stage of monopoly capital, most notably under the influence of Lenin (1963) in his *Imperialism* and elsewhere. This term is not to be identified with the formation of cartels and oligopoly as such, even though this is a characteristic of the stage. Rather it is the economic and related social phenomena associated with the centralization of capital that led machine production to be denoted as the stage of monopoly capital. We cannot enter here into Marx's reflections on these questions nor on how he thought that welfare and labour legislation might be established. We do note that in common with Smith, his analysis of the evolution of economic forces remains firmly embedded in these forces' relations to society as a whole.

Earlier we saw how Smith's analysis of the division of labour led to a particular understanding of the development of the relations between town and country as the basis for the development of capitalism. In the light of our subsequent discussion of Marx's theory of the division of labour, we can see that Smith sees this problem in terms of the development of exchange relations between town and country, as relations of exchange between one producer and another producer or consumer. He neglects, what is crucial for Marx, the development of exchange relations between capital and labour as classes, owning respectively the physical and the human means of production. In other words, what is crucial for Marx in the relationship between town and country in the emergence of capitalism is the creation of a class of wage-labourers dispossessed of means of production and free only to sell the commodity labour-power. Both writers agree that the division between town and country is the point of departure for the development of capitalism. Whereas Smith sees the expansion of this division through exchange as crucial, Marx argues that the dissolution of Smith's agricultural stage, feudalism, requires the dispossession of the peasantry from the land, a transformation of the relations of production in the countryside that may be stimulated but which cannot be brought about by exchange with the town. (For Marx's analysis see especially Part VII of *Capital I.*) It is this which explains Smith's difficulty in reconciling this natural order of development from country to town with his observation that exchange relations developed between the two without stimulating capitalist production sufficiently in Europe.

Finally, let us consider how Marx's theory of the division of labour led him to grasp certain critical insights into economic theory and ideology. The social division of labour as a relationship between commodities is a relationship between use values, things, which tends to obscure the underlying value relations between producers. This is the basis of commodity fetishism, treating relations between people as if they were limited to relations between things. As the division of labour develops in production the source of value and surplus value become more deeply obscured. First, increasing productivity is associated with the power of collective labour organized in co-operation for a division of labour that dulls the skills of many workers. There is nothing unique to capitalism in the power of collective labour, as the building of the pyramids illustrates. Nevertheless, capitalism does develop it to a fine and extensive art because wage-labour makes collective labour freely available. As it does so, it is capital that increasingly appears to be the source of wealth, since what is a gain for the productive power of capital through collective labour is a loss to the labourer in terms of eroded skills, functions and control. With the growing use of fixed and constant capital and the displacement of the labourer by machinery, labour as the source of value is increasingly denied. It is seen at best as one source of value among *other things*.

This is how the division of labour in production obscures the role of labour in the production of value and surplus value. In the social division of labour, the concealment is reinforced. The confinement of each worker to a particular task in a particular sector renders impossible a direct vision of the performance of surplus labour. As Smith observed, the day-labourer draws consumption from the expenditure of wages on the products of many industries and their associated labours whilst he remains confined to a single industry. No direct comparison can be made between the labour that he performs and the labour with which he is compensated in the form of products. This contrasts with feudal and slave societies in which the compulsion to perform surplus labour is more direct and apparent. As the social division of labour develops, so the source of profits in surplus labour becomes less transparent.

In addition, the growing division of labour is accompanied by differences between capitals both within and between sectors. There is a tendency for profits to be earned between sectors according to capital advanced, and the composition of capital advanced will vary across sectors. Consequently, as rates of profits are equalized by competition, capital (advanced) will be seen as the source of profits rather than labour's creation of surplus value.

Within a sector, differences in profitability will be associated with differences in the level of capital accumulation so that again capital can be considered to be the source of profits.

Consequently, the ideological significance of a growing division of labour is not confined to the role played in reifying economic and social relations. It also plays an importance role at the level of theory. In this, Smith is an early and outstanding illustration. For the rude society, Smith considers that a labour theory of value would suffice to explain the ratios at which products changed hands. In moving to the commercial stage he abandons a value theory based on labour-time. Given his exchange based orientation, Smith is unable to penetrate in his analysis to a value theory based on labour time once the phenomena associated with an increasing division of labour begin to develop. In its place, Smith substitutes a components theory of price, the idea that price is made up of the various independent component parts formed from wages, profits and rents. As it stands this is the most superficial and tautologous explanation of price formation. Yet Smith did not rely exclusively or even predominantly upon the static formulation of a price theory after finding labour as the source of value inadequate beyond a rude society. Rather, the developing division of labour is seen in a dynamic wealth creating context and so contributes independently to the formation of value. We take up this explanation of Smith's value theory later in chapter 5.

For the moment we contrast it with Marx's conclusions. He considers that his analysis of the division of labour confirms his value theory whilst he reveals that it obscures the role of value in the way that we have outlined. Capital accumulation drives the wedge deeper between the creation of value and surplus value and their formation in exchange as price and profit. Yet the developing division of labour as a relationship between capital and labour over production combines to demand a value theory based on labour-time. The transformation of the relations in production bring a hierarchy of skills, dulling of skills and the displacement of labour by machinery. The resulting heterogeneities are, nevertheless, still rendered homogeneous by the equivalence established between labours in the exchange of products as commodities. The compulsion to accumulate coerced by competition drives the labour to be performed as socially necessary labour-time. Certainly value relations become more complex with the more sophisticated development of the capitalist economy. For Marx this means a more sophisticated development of value theory not its abandonment. It is these issues that we take up in part in the next chapter whilst noting that they lie at the heart of the controversy over value theory and the so-called 'transformation problem'.

Further Reading

Marx devotes a considerable part of Volume I of *Capital* to a theoretical and empirical analysis of the development and significance of manufacture and machinery. See also the Appendix to Volume I, sometimes called the missing chapter VI, which sees this more abstractly as the transition from precapitalist to capitalist methods of production. In Volume I, Marx also develops a sophisticated analysis both of the role played by class struggle between capital and labour and of competition between capitals in producing the welfare legislation and conditions necessary to stimulate and consolidate the capitalist stage of machine production. For a discussion of this as the stage of monopoly capitalism, see chapter 7 of Fine and Harris: *Rereading Capital*, (1979). For descriptions of nineteenth century labour see M. Berg (ed.): *Technology and Toil in Nineteenth Century Britain* (1979), and for the twentieth century see Braverman: *Labour and Monopoly Capital* (1974).

The way in which capitalism is established is an important issue quite apart from its relation to the division of labour and the relations between town and country. It has relevance for the historical analysis of the origins of capitalism in what are now the advanced countries as well as for the theory of underdevelopment as capitalism emerges in the Third World.

Marx examined the historical origins of capitalism in Part VII of Volume I of *Capital* and also in various places in Volume III. He sees it as the dispossession of the peasantry from the land, a so-called 'primitive accumulation.' The process concerns a transformation of the existing relations of production rather than self-sacrificing abstinence on the part of capitalists. Capitalism has its origins in agriculture but the expansion of exchange there and with the town is a necessary but not determining element of the process.

Marx's analysis has itself been a subject of controversy within Marxism. A debate between Dobb and Sweezy, collected with other contributions in Hilton(ed.): *The Transition from Feudalism to Capitalism* (1976), in many ways reproduces the differences between Marx and Smith in terms of the relative importance of the roles of country and town and production and exchange in the development of capitalism. Brenner: 'The Origins of Capitalist Development: A Critique of Neo-Smithian Marxism' *New Left Review* (1977) shows that this debate has relevance for contemporary theory by demonstrating the proximity between Smith's analysis and that of current theories of unequal exchange as explanations of underdevelopment.

Smith's ideas concerning the division of labour are discussed by Meek and Skinner in 'The Development of Adam Smith's Ideas on the Division of Labour' *Economic Journal* (1973). There they show that the limiting extent of the market on the division of labour shot to prominence in Smith's thought as his lectures on economics evolved into *The Wealth of Nations*.

3
On Ricardo's Theory of Value

Value Theory in Ricardo

If the division of labour is the starting point for Smith's economics and a crucial element in Marx's analysis, the same importance does not exist for it within Ricardo's work. Indeed, in his *Principles of Political Economy and Taxation* there seem to be only two passing references to the division of labour and each of these takes for granted its association with an increasing productivity without further examination. This does not mean that the division of labour is absent from Ricardo's considerations. This is true only for the division of labour within the production process. The social division of labour is present in all but name in any theory that attempts to explain the ratio at which commodities exchange since commodity production generates the social division of labour along the lines of the market. Ricardo is concerned with the rate at which commodities exchange but by remaining silent on the division of labour whilst doing so, he sets a tradition that has subsequently been accepted almost without exception and without thought.

In his *Principles*, Ricardo begins in his Preface with the statement that 'to determine the laws which regulate . . . distribution, is the principal problem in Political Economy.' In attempting to do so, however, Ricardo first has to deal with the problem of value and this occupies the first chapter of the *Principles*. The crucial element in Ricardo's theory of value is his strong identification of its source with the quantity of labour employed in the production of commodities. This is a commitment to a value theory based on labour time which was to remain with him even unto his death-bed. The draft of a manuscript, the final version of which was being worked upon at the time of his death, closes as follows:

That the greater or less quantity of labour worked up in commodities can only be the only the cause of their alteration in value is completely made out as soon as we are agreed that all commodities are the produce of labour and would have no value but for the labour expended upon them. Though this is true it is still exceedingly difficult to discover or even to imagine any commodity which shall be perfect general

necessary but not sufficient.

measure of value, as we shall see by the observations that follow (*Collected Works*, IV, p. 397).

We shall take up Ricardo's difficulty of finding a perfect or standard measure of value later. For the moment we are concerned to clear the ground of certain possible confusions. Ricardo's work certainly does contain the notion that value is determined by labour-time of production. He also demonstrates, for reasons which will become clear, that the ratio at which commodities exchange tends to diverge from the ratios of these labour values. Such exchange ratios or exchange values are unfortunately termed values from time to time by Ricardo. At the very least then, there is a terminological confusion in Ricardo's presentation. But it is a confusion which goes beyond exposition, because it is Ricardo's commitment to labour as a source of value which leads him to wish to explain (exchange) value by the ratio of labour values. This he is unable to do. As a result, the distinction between value as measured by labour time and exchange value is certainly to be found in Ricardo but there is also an identification of the two to be found on occasion. This can happen in two ways. Exchange value can be identified with value so that commodities are presumed to exchange at their labour-time of production. Alternatively, value can be identified with exchange value, so that value is no longer determined by the labour-time of production.

Ricardo's confusion is created by a commitment to analyse the categories of the capitalist economy with an immediate confrontation of these with an analysis of values as measured by labour-time. It will be instructive to approach his theory by trying to see why he should retain this commitment to value, even as he found it inadequate. We shall do this by examining the problems that he posed himself for solution. Perhaps the most important of these is his need to criticize Adam Smith's components theory of price. Smith's theory is seen as an attempt to form price out of three independently determined elements of wages, profits and rents. We have touched on this briefly in the previous chapter and take it up in more detail in chapter 5. Smith's components theory leads to a false conclusion as far as Ricardo's theory is concerned. For Smith, an increase in wages would have the effect of increasing all prices to the extent that they bear a wage cost. For Ricardo, this is a nonsensical conclusion. Taking money to be the commodity gold, he can show that an increase in wages will affect all commodities so that to argue that all prices will increase, raises the question of an increase relative to what. Accordingly, Ricardo wishes to show that changes in wages do not affect the value of commodities. Rather, his view is that an increase in wages is compensated for by a decrease in profits so that commodities continue to exchange at their values.

Ricardo's argument against Smith is not simply technical. He observes that Smith derives his components theory as the economy emerges from the rude society. Accumulation leads to a division of net output between capital and labour in the form of profit and wages. This confuses Smith into believing that value itself must change as a result of this division. Ricardo's commitment to a concept of value based on labour-time allows him to see that the division or redivision of net product in no way affects the values of commodities. Consequently, there is nothing in the emergence of wages and profits as such which necessitates the abandoning of a value theory based on labour time.

Nevertheless there is an error in Ricardo's reasoning rather than Smith's at this stage of the debate. Ricardo's argument is tautologous. If commodities exchange at their values, then a change in the level of wages will not alter their exchange values because it will not have altered their values. The telling assumption is that commodities exchange at their values once a division occurs between profits and wages, and it is this assumption that Smith questions. Ricardo goes on to question the assumption himself by analysing the formation of exchange value. Profit is earnt in proportion to the time for which capital is advanced, the turnover time of capital. Two production processes may embody the same quantity of labour but if one is slower to come to the market for some systematic reason, such as a longer time taken in the production process, then it must command a higher price. For otherwise, its rate of profit per unit of time would be lower and capital would flow out of the sector.

Exactly the same argument applies to the different proportions in which capital is advanced as fixed and circulating capital. Machinery, tools and so on which comprise the first will be advanced for a longer period of time than the latter which is composed of wage and raw material payments. The price of a commodity must be greater, the larger is the proportion of fixed to circulating capital advanced. The basis for Ricardo's argument and the need for its modification in the light of the differing durabilities of capital is illustrated by the following:

He (Torrens) makes it appear that Smith says that after capital accumulates and industrious people are set to work the quantity of labour employed is not the only circumstance that determines the value of commodities, and that I oppose this opinion. Now I want to shew that I do not oppose this opinion in the way that he represents me to do so, but Adam Smith thought, that as in the early stages of society, all the produce of labour belonged to the labourer, and as after stock was accumulated, a part went to profits, that accumulation, necessarily, without any regard to the different degrees of durability of capital, or any other circumstance whatever, raised the prices of exchangeable value of commodities, and consequently that their value was no longer regulated by the quantity of labour necessary to their production. In opposition to him, I maintain that it is not because of this division into profits and wages, – it is not because capital accumulates, that exchangeable value varies, but it is in all stages of society, owing only to two causes: one of the more or less quantity of labour required, the other the greater or less durability of capital: – that the former is never superseded by the latter, but is only modified by it. (*Collected Works*, VII, p. 377, but see also Sraffa's *Introduction* to Volume I p. xxxvii.)

Ricardo shows within his own analysis that commodities do not exchange at their values once there are differences between capitals in their durability and in the proportions of fixed and circulating capital. Consequently, his challenge to Smith's theory has to be reformulated. Ricardo remains aware that the value produced by labour cannot be altered by its division between profits and wages but the ratios at which exchanges take place can be so altered. Accordingly, his problem becomes one of determining how the exchange values of commodities, which already diverge from their values, are altered by changes in wages. For a commodity which relies almost exclusively on the use of fixed capital, an increase of wages will bring a decline in its exchange value because the reduction in the rate of profit, which follows from the wage increase, will reduce the profits added to cost to make up price. Conversely, a commodity produced almost exclusively by labour will yield an increased price. Two conclusions can be drawn. The higher the turnover time and the composition of fixed to circulating capital, the more a commodity's exchange value has a tendency to decrease as wages increase. Those with a higher composition or durability will produce a lower price and vice versa. The movement away from an identification of value with exchange value implies a movement away from an absolute measure of exchange value, except by money, as labour-time as a source of (exchange) value is modified according to the time for which it has been advanced.

Apart from these complications, Ricardo can be quite happy with his conclusions for their critical contribution against Smith. Admittedly, prices do not remain the same when wages increase, but there cannot be a general price increase. Some prices will rise, just as others will fall. From the point of view of the critique of Smith, little is gained by modifying value as an explanation of exchange value according to differing turnover times and compositions of capital. Ricardo estimates that changes in wages are not liable to change relative prices by more than 6 or 7 per cent and he is content to work theoretically within the 7 per cent solution.

Changes in price, however, are governed by a number of factors. The most obvious is the choice of the commodity that is money. Even if value and exchange value are identical, changes in the labour-time required to produce the money commodity would change the prices of other commodities in proportion. Changes in the turnover time and in the durability of the capital used to produce the money commodity, even if labour-time of production remained the same, would also change the prices of other commodities. Changes in wages would affect prices according to the ratio of fixed and circulating capital for the commodities under consideration relative to that ratio for the money commodity. Prices then are governed in part by changes in the conditions under which the money commodity is produce and how these interact with changes in wages. Ricardo assumes for theoretical purposes that the conditions under which money is produced remain constant. This is in order that the changes in the conditions of production of other commodities can be measured by changes in prices without these being affected by changes in the conditions of production of gold.

There remains, however, the problem that the changes in prices of other commodities may result from changes in wages and not from changes in conditions of production. Ricardo is acutely aware of this problem and that it is not subject to exact theoretical solution. As observed earlier, he is content to adopt an empirical or more exactly an approximate solution. This means finding a money commodity for which the variations in prices from relative values will in general be least extreme when wages change. He fixes upon a commodity produced with an average composition of fixed and circulating capital as a standard measure of value and makes it money. This guarantees that the ratio of fixed to circulating capital of any other commodity will not too severely diverge from that of the money commodity and changes in prices will more or less reflect changes in conditions of production. In his section on an invariable measure of value, Ricardo concludes in the *Principles*:

Neither gold then, nor any other commodity, can ever be a perfect measure of value for all things; but as I have already remarked, that the effect on the relative prices of things, from a variation in profits, is comparatively slight; that by far the most important effects are produced by the varying quantities of labour required for production, and therefore, if we suppose this important cause of variation removed from the production of gold, we shall possess as near an approximation to a standard measure of value as can be theoretically conceived. May not gold be considered as a commodity produced with such proportions of the two kinds of capital as approach nearest to the average quantity employed in the production of most commodities? May not these proportions be so nearly equally distant from the two extremes, the one where little fixed capital is used, the other where little labour is employed, as to form a just mean between them?

It is crucial that Ricardo's solution is an approximate one and further that theoretically there is no exact solution. The divergence between value and exchange value follows from the divergence between ratios of fixed and circulating capital. These ratios in turn reflect differences in the ratios between past and present labour. There is no way in which the two dimensional character of fixed (past) and circulating (present) capital (labour) can be reduced to a single dimension independently of knowledge of the rate of profit that makes the reduction. This is Ricardo's heavily emphasized point in his last manuscript where he compares the measure of length with the measure of value, the difference being the impossibility of an absolute standard for the latter. Consequently, Ricardo's standard of value cannot be established accurately prior to a knowledge of distribution because of the need to measure the relative value of past and present labour. Because commodities are exchanged at ratios reflecting the division between past and present labour in their production, an absolute standard of value becomes impossible. For, if it did exist, it would reconcile the irreconcilable, that is one-dimensional measure of a two-dimensional quantity: past and present labour.

Ricardo then is correct to find that only an approximate solution to the standard is possible. But this solution itself creates a paradox. Theoretically, we know that no absolute standard of value is possible. For practical purposes, however, we adopt a measure through a money produced under the average composition. On this basis we compare the relative values of commodities by the absolute standard created by labour-time. Ricardo's approximation to relative exchange values appears to have produced an absolute standard of value. Labour exerted in the past and present according to the average composition shall count as an absolute standard of value in general. Of course, the result is to return to a position in which the exchange value of any two commodities, whether one is money or not, will be in the ratio of their labour-time of production. The use of a money of average composition is intended to minimize the potential inaccuracies resulting from taking prices to reflect production changes when in fact they could be reflecting wage changes. A further complication is that wage changes produce price changes from prices that already diverge from values. But Ricardo is more concerned with the former changes since he wishes to criticize Smith's proposition of a positive relation between all prices and a wage increase. The result is that Ricardo uses and at times searches for an absolute and invariable standard of value when he has already shown it to be impossible as a direct explanation of exchange value.

To summarize: what we find in Ricardo's theory, both in its finished versions and during the course of its development, is a tension between labour as the source of value in production and capital advanced as the source of value in exchange. The more value and exchange value are identified the greater is a tension which can only be eased in Ricardo's theory by introducing other sources of value than labour-time. Yet Ricardo remains committed to the notion that labour-time is the source of value, and that other factors only modify this principle. Consequently his difficulties persist.

Marx's Critique of Ricardo

As we have seen Ricardo failed to distinguish value and exchange value adequately, and this is a starting point for Marx's critique of Ricardo's value theory. There are, however, many aspects to this critique. To begin with, Ricardo does not consciously utilize different levels of abstraction within his theory and this is why value and exchange value can at times be taken to be identical. On the other hand, precisely because he confronts the appearances of the capitalist economy with the concept of value, Ricardo does employ abstraction within his theory for which value plays an underlying role. Yet Marx's concept of value differs from Ricardo's even though the labour theory of value is often thought of as being associated with a Ricardo-Marx duo. For Ricardo, the concept of value is ahistorically defined by the labour-time embodied in commodities. This is why he can engage in a debate with Smith over whether the development from a rude to a capitalist society will modify the determination of value, whereas commodity production is in reality absent from rude society.

For Marx, value is created by social relations before it can be a result of the expenditure of labour-time. These social relations must include the organization of the economy so that products take the form of commodities. There must be production for exchange. One consequence of this is that the different types of labour in different sectors of the economy, what Marx termed concrete labours, are brought into equivalence with each other by the equivalence that is established between commodities as use-values. Whatever the numerical content of this equivalence, its social content is that concrete labours are made to conform to a standard through exchange, giving rise to the existence of what Marx termed abstract labour. It is this relationship between concrete and abstract labour that forms the basis for Marx's concept of value. Value is created in production by concrete labour but owes its existence to the exchange relations that bring it into equivalence with other concrete labours as abstract labour. In Marx's theory then there can be no confusion between value as it is determined in production and the exchange value by which the value is represented in exchange. In addition, Marx's theory incorporates an historical and social content by demonstrating that the value concept is valid only for societies ruled by commodity production. We do not take up here the distinction between value produced by petty commodity production as opposed to capitalist commodity production. We do note however that such a distinction is unimportant for the value concept of Ricardo (and Smith) which is ahistorical and general, formed from the labour-times of production that prevail in any society irrespective of whether society itself has a mechanism for bringing these labour-times into equivalence. Consequently, this concept of value is imposed upon the analysis.

Marx's critique of Ricardo's value theory can begin at this conceptual level but it can be carried further. At times, Ricardo is forced to distinguish value and exchange value and, in doing so, he begins to abandon value itself. The pressure upon Ricardo to do this results from the introduction of profits and wages into his theory. Yet, just as value and exchange value are quite distinct, so are profits and surplus value, the one being the form of the other in exchange. Now, profit is created in Ricardo's theory by the payment to workers of wages which represent less labour-time than they contribute. Consequently, it concerns a relationship between capital and

[right margin handwritten annotations:] FUNDAMENTAL DIFFERENCE BETWEEN RICARDO'S AND MARX' THEORIES OF VALUE

Difference between Profit and surplus Value.

labour over the time worked. On the other hand, profit is earnt within Ricardo's theory according to capital advanced, and this involves a relationship between capitalists in competition. For Marx, Ricardo's first notion of profit corresponds to surplus value, which has to be distinguished from profit proper, the form in which surplus value as a whole is distributed to individual capitalists according to capital advanced in exchange. At this stage, we can summarize Marx's critique of Ricardo in terms of the label with which he dubbed him, the best representative of bourgeois scientific political economy. Ricardo is scientific for his commitment to a value theory based on labour-time, the category essential for an analysis of a capitalist economy dominated by commodity production. He is bourgeois for taking the forms of value (and surplus value) in exchange for granted, thereby confusing them with their origins in production and according them an equal conceptual status with the underlying value concepts.

It may appear that the only difference between Marx and Ricardo over the production of surplus value is that the latter confuses surplus value with profit. This view is supported by their both taking the level of wages to contain a moral and historical element. However, Ricardo's theory of wages and their relation to profit is based almost on a technical definition alone. Labour is able to produce more than is required for subsistence reproduction. In Marx's theory, the divergence between what labour consumes and what labour produces is the result of a social relation between capital and labour, not a technical relation. There is an exchange between capital and labour over the level of wages but it is not labour that is bought and sold. Rather, it is the commodity labour-power, the ability to work, which is sold for the wage and capitalists must compel labourers to work beyond the value embodied in the wage, whatever that level be. The compulsion to perform surplus labour derives from the monopoly ownership of the means of production by capital and the freedom of the worker to sell labour-power, a freedom which implies both no ties to other non-capitalist exploiters as well as a freedom from ownership and access to the means of production. The source of surplus value then does not lie in labour being sold at a wage below its value. Indeed, the value of labour is a nonsensical expression since labour, in the appropriate social relations, is value itself. Surplus value arises from the compulsion on the labourer to work beyond the time represented by the value of labour-power.

The confusion within Ricardo's theory arises when the division of net produce between capital and labour is taken in conjunction with the division between fixed and circulating capital. That Ricardo's problems originate in this way is important for a number of reasons. First, because a distinction is drawn between labour performed in the past and labour performed in the present, the divergence between value and exchange value can be deduced. Second, it is deduced in the simplest way. Despite the introduction of differing compositions and durabilities of capital, these are both reducible to a common measure, the time for which capital has been advanced. In Ricardo's theory it is as if all labour is either performed at some average fixed date in the past or is performed in the present. Accordingly, production has become a two-sector affair with past and present labour as the two inputs. The (exchange) value of products can only be calculated if there is a relative evaluation of these two inputs. This evaluation corresponds to the rate of profit which is in turn determined once the level of wages is fixed. Third, to maintain this simplification it is best to treat circulating capital as if it is purely hiring labour and does not contain any raw materials. For these embody labour expended in the past, potentially at different dates than that represented by the average. Ricardo does tend to analyse the divergence between value and exchange value as if no raw materials are used. Consequently, his focus is on the differing durabilities and compositions of capital, between fixed and circulating capital. In contrast, modern treatments of the relationship between value and price tend to focus on the differing compositions of the value of raw materials to hired labour.

Marx criticizes Ricardo for failing to distinguish or focus on the difference between constant and variable capital rather than on the difference between fixed and circulating capital. This criticism has to be interpreted carefully and certainly not literally. Unfortunately, Marx's views on other economists are mainly to be found in *Theories of Surplus Value*, the fourth volume of Capital, which was never finally prepared for publication and suffers from abruptness, lack of clarity and disorganization.

Consequently, Marx's criticism of Ricardo is not that the latter believes that the only form embodied labour can take is fixed capital. Rather, Ricardo tends to present the divergence of exchange value from value in the context of the distinction between fixed and circulating capital in which the constant capital of raw materials is excluded from the latter. This allows Ricardo to avoid the problem of the divergence of the exchange value of raw materials from their value and to reduce the economy to a two-sector one in labour-time. Ricardo can then examine the effects of wage changes on the changes in the (exchange) value of commodities with differing compositions and durabilities of capital, prior to his having established what those variations from value would be as a result of the differing compositions and durabilities themselves. To settle that question would have required a proper distinction between value and exchange value and consequently to a distinction between that advance of capital that has its value preserved and that which adds surplus value. So whilst Ricardo's distinction between fixed and circulating capital can raise the problem of the divergence between value and exchange value, it cannot solve it. In addition, since the distinction is made in exchange according to the time at which a (labour) advance is made, the source of profits becomes to be identified with a capital advance rather than with the performance of surplus labour.

Marx's criticism of Ricardo's failure to distinguish constant and variable capital and his confusion of them with fixed and circulating capital is itself confused by another issue in Marx's assessment of Ricardo. Because Ricardo identifies surplus value with profits, his analysis of profit is in fact an analysis of surplus value for the conditions in which capital employs labour alone, when constant capital is zero. Elsewhere Ricardo also has a tendency to treat changes in wages, and hence surplus value, as if they were the sole cause of changes in the rate of profit. This is true of his analysis of corn production, for which the corn-labour ratio remains constant in production as productivity declines with the movement into worse lands. Ricardo's discussion of movements in the rate of profit are dominated by the movements in surplus value with a tendency to exclude the influence made by a changing composition of constant to variable capital.

There is a complex relationship then between Ricardo's theory and Marx's critique of it. Ricardo uses categories that have an explanatory power but in a confusing and misleading way. We began with the conflation of value and exchange value. It becomes a confusion between profit and surplus value which is in turn related to the distinction made between fixed and circulating rather than constant and variable capital. Not that Marx considers the distinction between fixed and circulating capital unimportant. It is simply not appropriate for confronting the problem of the divergence between value and exchange value: the reflection of the distinction between the production of surplus value by living labour and its distribution according to capital advanced. For Marx, the difference between fixed and circulating capital effects this distribution but the distinction is more important for the relationship between the credit system and the cycle of production for which the different turnover times of production and of fixed capital are significant. However this belongs to the analysis of the cycle of production and of the credit system and not to the production and distribution of surplus value as such.

The Relation of Ricardian to Sraffian Economics

In his book *Production of Commodities By Means of Commodities*, Piero Sraffa has shown the existence of a standard commodity with certain properties. It is easy to interpret this commodity to be the one for which Ricardo searches as the invariable standard. In this regard, as in many other matters, Sraffa himself has been more cautious than his followers. In this section, we shall examine the extent to which Sraffa's standard commodity can be identified with Ricardo's invariable standard.

Essential to Sraffa's standard commodity is the notion of basic inputs. These are ones which are either used directly or indirectly in the production of every other commodity. The importance of the basics is that they form the basis on which the price, wage and profit relations are calculated. The prices of non-basics are derived from these relations, since their cost of production depends only upon the prices of the basic inputs plus profit and not upon their own price. The system of basics then provides a set of simultaneous equations between their own prices alone and the levels of wages and profits. Sraffa defines the standard commodity in terms of the system of basics. It is the composite commodity, a bundle of commodities, which if used in production as inputs would reproduce itself in the same proportions as outputs but on a larger scale. The simplest standard commodity is to be found in a one good world. If corn alone is used to produce corn, then it is the standard commodity. This is a convenient economy in which to analyse distribution since advances as capital, wages and profits can all be measured in corn. For a more heterogeneous economy, capital, wages and profits may be made up of bundles of commodities in different proportions so that there is no way of measuring distribution immediately upon a one-dimensional scale.

The standard commodity reduces the many commodity economy to one as if it were a corn-corn economy. If the economy were to use the standard commodity as advances and in which to pay wages, then the bundles of output and net output would be in the same proportions as the bundles of advances and wages, so that again each and every one can be measured along a one-dimensional scale. If the standard commodity were used as *numeraire*, a simple inverse relation exists between the level of wages and the rate of profit, reflecting the division of the net product between capital and labour. One important property then of the standard commodity is that it reduces the economy to one as if it were a corn-corn economy at least as far as the problem of distributing net product is concerned.

The standard commodity is defined purely in terms of the basic inputs excluding labour. Labour is treated as a separate input which is paid a wage according to the distribution of net product. The labour embodied in a commodity consists of living labour expended in the present and the past labour that has been exercised to produce the physical inputs used in the present. These inputs have themselves been produced by living labour in the previous period together with other inputs. These inputs have been produced by living labour of the previous period . . . and so on. Any one commodity then is associated with a sequence of dated labours running back into the indefinite past. Suppose this sequence is represented by ℓ_0, $\ell_1, \ell_2, \ldots \ldots$

The price of a commodity embodying this profile of present and past labour will be given by $w(\ell_0 + \ell_1(1+r) + \ell_2(1+r)^2 + \ldots .)$ where w is the wage and r the rate of profit since the wage cost of labour expended i years ago $w\ell_i$ has been advanced for i years and must yield a profit compounded for i years at the rate r, $w\ell_i(1+r)^i$. When the wage increases, the rate of profit decreases so that the effect on the commodity's price is ambiguous, since the increasing wage cost is offset by a lower rate of profit at which past costs are being discounted. In addition, the commodity in which wages are being expressed, the *numeraire*, is itself the product of a profile of present and past labours, so that the prices of other commodities will reflect not only their own profile of labour costs but also those of the *numeraire*.

The standard commodity has been considered to have the property of eliminating this second source of variation because of the special way in which the profile of past labour is layered. Since, as a set of outputs, it is the product of inputs in the same proportion, the quantity of labour used one year ago will be in inverse proportion to the rate of increase of outputs over inputs, say $\ell_1 = t\,\ell_0$. Similarly, the labour used two years ago will be in exactly the same inverse proportion to that used one year ago, $\ell_2 = t\,\ell_1$. It follows that the profile of dated labour is $\ell = \ell_0,\ t\ell,\ t^2\ell,\ t^3\ell,\ \ldots\ldots$ where $t < 1$ is the ratio of inputs to outputs for the standard commodity. Labour used in a previous period is a constant proportion of that used the period before. By contrast, the labour profile of any other commodity would be higgledy-piggledy and this is the source of a complicated price variation with wage (and profit) variation. The use of the standard commodity as *numeraire* eliminates the variation in relative prices due to the uneven layering of its labour and places it all upon the layering of labour of the commodity under consideration.

The identification of Sraffa's standard commodity with Ricardo's invariable standard could easily be made. For each there is a relationship between past and present labour. These cause variations in prices due to wage changes. Each theory constructs an 'average' commodity. Here, however, the similarities end. This is perhaps most clear when it is realized that there are no basic commodities in Ricardo's system, and hence there can be no Sraffian standard commodity within it.

For Sraffa, commodities are produced by commodities (with labour), and these commodities have been produced by other commodities and so on back in time indefinitely. The same is not true for Ricardo. Usually, he thinks of commodities as being produced by labour alone. When he refines this, he does so by dividing this labour into two sorts. There is living labour expended in the present and past labour reduced on average to an equivalent amount expended in the previous period. One way in which Ricardo represents this division of labour is in terms of past labour to form fixed capital expended in this period as circulating capital. For these reasons, the apparent congruity between the theories in using past and present labour is in fact more significant for the different methods employed. Sraffa's sequence of dated labour is an ideal construction, extending as it does into the indefinite past. Ricardo, on the other hand, is attempting to reconcile the coexistence of capital and labour with the latter as the sole source of value. Consequently, Ricardo's dated labour can only extend back one period as an approximation to a *finite* sequence of dated labours, whereas dated labour, linked by Sraffa to the production of commodities by commodities, must less realistically extend back indefinitely.

This difference between the two theories of labour in Sraffa and Ricardo produce a sharp difference in their solutions to the search for an invariable standard. Ricardo emphasizes and demonstrates that his search for an invariable standard is not subject to exact theoretical solution but is only amenable to a more or less accurate empirical approximation. In contrast, Sraffa's standard commodity has an exact theoretical solution. Nothing could better illustrate the difference between the two theories.

However, it could be argued that the Sraffian standard commodity is the solution to the perfection of Ricardo's economics just as the Sraffian system solves the price problems that troubled Ricardo. Such an interpretation depends upon eliminating the value element within Ricardo's work in so far as it depends upon labour-time alone. This can be done but we have attempted to show that it does not correspond to the spirit of Ricardo's analysis. As always, the Sraffian system attempts to displace the role played by labour in value theory and substitute for it an analysis in terms of use values, technical coefficients, inputs, commodities or whatever.

Sraffa is himself unclear about the relationship between Ricardo's standard and his own (see Sraffa (1973), p. 94), noting only parallels between the two. In another regard, the standard as a means of measuring distribution, he has been more direct. The standard commodity reduces the economy to one as if it were a corn-corn economy so that the distributional relations between capital and labour can be simply treated in terms of the division of net product. The standard commodity then serves two purposes, providing a commodity with a uniform layering of dated labour and one by which distribution can be simply analysed. The two purposes are intimately related and are achieved simultaneously by the standard commodity. It becomes natural to search for the same dual purpose for Ricardo's invariable standard, especially as he is both concerned with distributional relations and analyses their evolution through the development of productivity in a corn dominated economy. Sraffa himself suggests that Ricardo might have this purpose in mind, although the evidence for this is flimsy and must be stretched to the limits. Sraffa admits:

This argument is never stated by Ricardo in any of his extant letters and papers, he must have formulated it either in his lost 'papers on the profits of capital' of March 1814, or in conversation, since Malthus opposes him in the following terms which are no doubt an echo of Ricardo's own formulation . . . (Introduction to *Principles*, p. xxxi).

A more plausible interpretation rejects the view that, because two problems are both solved by the standard commodity in the Sraffian system, the same problems exist within Ricardo's system and are to be solved by his invariable standard. We have already shown that Ricardo's and Sraffa's systems diverge and with them, so diverge the standard commodity and the invariable standard. Ricardo's analysis of the corn economy can, however, be seen as a highly simplified Sraffian economy in which the only basic is corn. But then, in so far as Ricardo sees corn as a special case of a composite commodity representing an invariable standard for distribution (and the evidence for this is slight), it is an invariable standard that differs from the one confronting the need for approximation in the divergence of exchange value from value. More likely is that Ricardo takes his approximation of exchange value by value to justify an analysis of productivity and distribution in terms of labour-time, a return to his instinctive commitment. Indeed, in his presentation of the corn-economy, Ricardo tends to see production taking place through the advance of capital and labour as before rather than through the advance of corn and labour.

We have tried to show that the identification of the Sraffian standard commodity with the Ricardian invariable standard imposes a false Sraffian interpretation upon Ricardo's economics. Ricardo's perpetual struggle is to identify value, measured by labour-time, as the source of exchange value. The Sraffian system attempts to identify exchange value with a physical system of use-values in which the standard commodity reduces the economy to the simplest form of *physical* reproduction. Sraffa himself notices that by doing so capitalism is treated by theoretical analogy with Physiocracy, a school of economic thought concerned with the physical agricultural surplus (Sraffa (1973), p. 93). This should serve warning that the 'cornifying' of the capitalist economy is a theoretical 'devaluing' and the introduction of ahistorical elements of analysis, for the production of commodities does not take place by commodities but by labour.

Further Reading

There is no substitute for reading the first chapter of Ricardo's *Principles*. The introduction by Sraffa is excellent although he does tend to bend his interpretation of Ricardo towards his own system based on commodities (use values) rather than values (labour-time). For a discussion of the differences between Marx's and other theories of value based on labour time, see my *Economic Theory and Ideology* (1980), chapter 6, and also chapter 5 for a critique of Sraffian economics. For a more sophisticated treatment of Marx's theory of value, see Elson(ed.): *Value: The Representation of Labour in Capitalism* (1979). Broome gives an exposition of the standard commodity in 'Sraffa's Standard Commodity', *Australian Economic Papers*, (1977) and shows that Sraffa remains confused over the nature of the standard commodity in 'The Allegedly Invariable Value of Sraffa's Standard Commodity', *Birkbeck Discussion Paper*, No. 64, (1978).

4
Ricardo and Marx on the Formation of Rent

Differential Rent

Ricardo's preoccupation with the theory of distribution would necessarily lead him to formulate a theory of rent. But this subject cannot be confined to distribution alone. As we shall see here and also in later chapters, rent theory is intimately related to value theory. In line with the Sraffian 'cornification' of Ricardo's theory, an approach we have criticized in the previous chapter, it has become traditional to present Ricardo's theory of rent in terms of a corn-corn model in which all means of production and of consumption are reduced to the single commodity corn. We will follow this tradition here, although we will indicate occasionally where Ricardo's own presentation diverges from the tradition.

For Ricardo, corn is a crucially important commodity because it serves as the major component in subsistence wages. The accumulation of profits will add to the demand for labour and so wages will rise and with them the demand for corn. This will have two effects. The supply of corn can only be provided by the extension of agriculture onto worse lands as far as fertility and location are concerned. Productivity in agriculture will decline and the price of corn will rise. Following Malthusian population theory, increased wages will stimulate population growth as long as they exceed physical subsistence in real terms. The tendency for accumulation to drive wages up is mitigated by an increase of labour supply from population growth. On the other hand, the declining productivity in agriculture raises the price of corn and with it the wage equivalent of physical subsistence. Consequently, wages cannot fall to their former level, despite highly co-operative population growth, because of the increasing subsistence costs of production.

The whole argument can be reformulated in value terms, as measured by labour time of production. As accumulation proceeds, the demand for labour increases the value of wages and the demand for corn. The labour force expands and with it the supply of corn but only at an increasing value as worse land is taken into cultivation. The value of subsistence wages also rises so that even if wages are held at subsistence levels by population growth, the rate of profit falls because of its inverse relation to the value of wages.

So far nothing has been said about rent. Indeed, the arguments, whatever their virtues, are quite independent of rent. Where rent does enter is in the precise formation of the value of corn. In Ricardo's theory, the value of corn is determined on the worst land in use. As a result of competition from idle land, the worst land can bear no rent. Capital employed there must, nevertheless, enjoy a normal, equalized rate of profit, otherwise capital would be withdrawn. The result is that a surplus is produced on the better lands and this is appropriated by the landowners as a differential rent.

The theory can be illustrated by a simple graph (see Diagram 1). Along the x-axis is marked the quantity of capital that has been accumulated. It is measured in 'doses' of corn for sowing and corn for wages which remain in fixed proportions. Ricardo himself tended to analyse these advances in terms of a quantity of capital rather than in physical terms. On the y-axis we mark net output. The two graphs represent average product AP and marginal product MP. Both graphs decline as the doses of capital applied increase since productivity declines in the movement onto worse lands. The marginal product actually measures that decline directly, but the average product only indirectly since it is averaged with the outputs of the previously used better lands. This is why the average is higher than the marginal product. The horizontal line at S represents the corn subsistence wage.

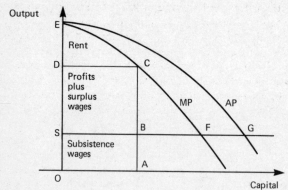

Diagram 1.   Ricardo's falling rate of profit.

Now suppose capital has been accumulated upto the point A. Then the worst land in use has marginal product AC and this determines the price of corn. The other better lands have surplus products represented by the distances between EC (the MP curve) and DC, the current output on the worst land. The area ECD then measures the total differential rent. The area

OABS measures the total subsistence requirements of workers since it is the level of subsistence multiplied by workers employed (proportional to the capital employed OA). As total net output is given by OACE (the sum of marginal products on all lands), SBCD remains to pay profits and any wages above subsistence that are brought about by labour shortage. In fact, SBCD represents the surplus that can be made available for subsequent capital advances and which moves A (and B and C) to the right over time.

As this happens, profits eventually become squeezed, although rents rise all the time as differentials between better and the worst land in use increase. Ultimately, the economy comes to rest at the stationary state F. There the worst land is just producing sufficient output to pay subsistence wages. Profits have disappeared altogether and the surplus on better lands accrues entirely in the form of rent (given by EFS). As there are no excess wages, population will have grown to the level appropriate to the extent of capital accumulation and simply reproduce itself at subsistence levels.

The model need not be as simple as it has been presented here. Profits may be driven to a minimum necessary to induce investment rather than to zero. Ricardo suggests a number of modifications himself. To some extent, manufacturers can be substituted for corn as part of the subsistence wage so that diminishing returns in agriculture can be displaced by constant or increasing returns. But there are limits to the reduction of corn consumption. Capital may also be applied intensively in two or more doses on a single land rather than extensively and uniformly from better to worst lands. Then the value of corn will be determined by the output associated with the application of the last least productive dose of capital which may not be on the worst land. This means that the worst land in use would bear a differential rent if its output is superior to the intensive margin. Nevertheless, on the assumption that the intensive margin is itself subject to diminishing returns, little will have changed. It is as if any land on which another dose of capital is applied is counted as a new land which just happens to coincide spatially with the old one. In short, there can be no reprieve for the class that provides the means of growth through the accumulation of profits. These will be eroded. Even if all rents were reinvested the stationary state would only be postponed to the point G at which workers are consuming the entire net product at subsistence wages. Foreign trade can also postpone the stationary state by transferring the extensive margin abroad.

There are some important consequences of Ricardo's analysis that do not emerge clearly from the technical considerations. Of these the most significant is that the determination of differential rent is independent of the system or pattern of landownership. The rents are calculated purely from differences in the productivity of different lands, or more exactly of capitals applied to the lands. All the system of landed property can do is to assign these rents to the owners of the lands concerned. Put another way,

Ricardo's theory of rent is quite independent of the conditions governing access of capital to the land. As far as the land is concerned, access is assumed, most explicitly in the conclusion that the last application of capital to the land pays no rent. Nevertheless, rents are paid to landlords, but these are determined much more by agreement amongst capitalist farmers than by agreement between capital and land over the conditions of access. The capitalist agree that each should earn an equal rate of profit as a result of competition amongst themselves. Those that have the better lands have to forego extra profits as differential rents. In Ricardo's theory then, high or low rents are the result of a high or low price of corn on the margin. There can be no rent component part of price except through monopoly increases in the price of corn.

Ricardo's theory has such a simplicity that there is no difficulty finding references explicitly illustrating his views. Chapter 2 of the *Principles* begins by attempting to relate rent to natural properties: 'Rent is that portion of the produce of the earth, which is paid to the landlord for the use of the original and indestructible powers of the soil (p. 67). Even this creates difficulties for Ricardo and he modifies his definition in a later chapter to define rent in terms of indestructible powers whether they are original or not. This is done to take account of investments which may have become historically consolidated into the qualities of the land under consideration. This is not of direct concern to us here but we will touch on this problem later.

Ricardo argues that agriculture production necessarily progresses from the most favourable to worsening conditions but begins by only tying this loosely to value formation:

The most fertile, and most favourably situated land will be first cultivated, and the exchangeable value of its produce will be adjusted in the same manner as the exchangeable value of all other comodities, by the total quantity of labour necessary in various forms, from first to last, to produce it, and bring it to market. When land of an inferior quality is taken into cultivation, the exchangeable value of raw produce will rise, because more labour is required to produce it (p. 72).

However, later, the value of corn is tied to the margin and with it, rent becomes price determined as a differential rather than contributing towards price:

The reason then, why raw produce rises in comparative value, is because more labour is employed in the production of the last portion obtained, and not because a rent is paid to the landlord. The value of corn is regulated by the quantity of labour bestowed on its production on that quality of land, or with that portion of capital, which pays no rent. Corn is not high because a rent is paid, but a rent is paid because corn is high; . . .

Ricardo then immediately asserts that these principles hold irrespective of the ownership of the land:

and it has been justly observed, that no reduction would take place in the price of corn, although landlords should forego the whole of the rent. Such a measure would only enable some farmers to live like gentlemen, but would not diminish the quantity of labour necessary to raise raw produce on the least productive land in cultivation (p. 74).

In other words, rents foregone by landlords would simply accrue to the thereby gentrified farmers. But Ricardo has failed to consider how these lucky gentlemen are to be selected for their good fortunes. In the absence of the rent payment, it is not done through the market. Without specifying how it is to be done, the idea that conditions of production remain unaltered on the worst land in use, if it were still to be the worst land in use, becomes questionable. That is, except for Ricardo, for whom land and capital in use and their associated rent and price information are independent of the system of landownership and are technically determined by conditions of fertility and location.

Finally, Ricardo denies the possibility of rent as a component part of price, except as a temporary monopoly price, unless all land is fully in use and price is determined by willingness to pay rather than by costs of production (see Chapter XXIV of the *Principles* which criticizes Adam Smith). We take up this denial of an absolute rent component to price in chapters 5 and 7.

Marx's Critique of Ricardo

Ricardo's analysis of rent has been considered a one good corn-corn theory because of the role played by agriculture in determining the rate of profit. Ricardo's motivation might be considered to be slightly different. Prior to an examination of rent, he attempts to establish and justify a theory of value based on labour-time. Despite his lack of success, Ricardo's rent theory is based on the continued identification of value with exchange value, and consequently with the failure to distinguish surplus value and profit. Because Ricardo wishes to explain the category of rent whilst remaining true to a value theory based on a labour-time and a profit theory based on capital advanced, he is led into further inconsistencies. These form the basis for Marx's criticism of Ricardian rent theory.

Rent arises in Ricardo's theory because of the differential productivities of equal capitals applied to lands of differing fertility. Consequently, individual agricultural capitals have different individual values, so that at whatever price corn is fixed, these capitals will yield different quantities of surplus value. What is necessary to Ricardo's rent theory is that individual capitals, in competition within a sector, yield a value of output that is determined by the least productive capital. Whether this is the case or not, competition within the sector has the affect of equalizing rates of profit within the sector so that the differential surpluses that exists between capitals on the land do not accrue to the capitals but are spirited away in the form of rent. Rents exist then because of surplus profits within the sector of agriculture.

For consistency, Ricardo should also allow the possibility of different productivities between capitals within other sectors. But this would raise two problems. How would value be formed in these sectors and who would appropriate the surplus profits? If value is not determined at the margin, the last capital employed in the sector would not be earning the equalized normal rate of profit across sectors. Whether value is determined at the margin or not, there will be different rates of profit formed within the sector according to the different levels of productivity. There will be no landlord to cream off these surplus profits as in the case of agricultural rents. Ricardo's theory of rent then depends upon an unequal treatment of agricultural and industrial capital as sectors as a whole and an unequal treatment of each within the sector. Agricultural capitals have unequal productivities but equal rates of profit, industrial capitals either have equal productivities or unequal rates of profit.

Marx locates the source of Ricardo's problems in his treatment of competition. Marx himself carefully distinguishes between competition within and competition between sectors. Competition within a sector establishes what Marx calls the market value in that sector out of capitals with differing productivities. The value will correspond in general to what becomes the normally established technique. Those with a higher or lower individual value will receive profits below or above the normal respectively. Competition between sectors establishes a tendency to equalize rates of profits but does so by redistributing surplus value as a whole between sectors in the form of profit according to capital advanced. Prices of production are thereby formed which diverge from values. What Ricardo does is to identify market value with exchange value and surplus value with the individual profits produced by each capital. Differential rent can then be formed within the agriculture sector alone by imposing the condition of equal profitability on that sector and shaking out the surplus profits as rents.

Ricardo does not examine how these results are a modification of the formation of value in the absence of land since he has not dealt with the divergence of individual values from value within a sector except in the presence of land. Nor does he examine how the results are a modification of the exchange of commodities at prices of production that diverge from values, since the surplus value produced in a sector immediately becomes profit and does not contribute to a common pool for redistribution between sectors. These problems form the point of departure for Marx's theory of rent from Ricardo's.

Marx's Theory of Agricultural Rent

Marx's treatment of rent does not begin with the theoretical conundrums that are produced by Ricardo's analysis. For Marx, rent must be examined in terms of the specific historical and empirical circumstances in which it is created. The process of value formation within agriculture will be modified by the intervention of landed property according to the conditions under which capital is allowed access to the land. The level of rents will be effected by different quality lands but these natural conditions do not determine rents. Prior consideration must be given to the nature of the relationship between landed property and capital. Consequently, there can be no technical determination of rent independent of the form of landed property and there can be no general theory of rent. Without the incorporation of an historical element into the theory, the determination of value within the rent yielding sector and its distinctiveness from other sectors becomes arbitrary or problematic as in Ricardo's theory.

Marx initially takes as the historical conditions for his analysis that the capitalist mode of production be fully established but that it be confronted by landed property as a condition of access to the land. His theory then appears to follow Ricardo's quite closely. For the application of equal capitals to unequal lands, market value within the sector will be determined on the worst land in use and differential rent will accrue to those landlords owning the better lands. Marx calls this differential rent of the first type. We denote it by DRI. There are, however, some important differences between Marx and Ricardo. In Ricardo's theory, these rents are a property of the land rather than of landed property. In contrast, for the rents to be admitted in Marx's theory, landlords must be shown to exist and to be powerful enough to intercept the surplus profits that are created by the application of the capitals to the different lands. For otherwise, a different system of access to the land will prevail and only by considering that in detail can the process of value and rent formation be formulated. Ricardo's rents are derived from the indestructible (and at times original) powers of the land, whereas a necessary condition for Marx's DRI is that the surplus profits associated with different lands should not be eroded by economic and/or social change.

The major difference between the two, however, is that Ricardo's analysis begins and closes with the principles of differential rent determined by differences in natural fertility. True, he does also consider an intensive margin, but this can be seen as merely treating one piece of land as if it were available for cultivation two or more times. By contrast, Marx's analysis of rent is only just beginning with the disclosure of DRI. This can best be seen in terms of the divergence between the two over the theory of value. Ricardo has quite happily explained rent whilst remaining true to a value theory based on labour-time. In doing so, he has avoided two problems that he has himself implicitly raised. The first is how market values are formed in industry in particular sectors when individual values or productivities diverge. The second is how prices of production that diverge from values effect the formation of rent. Marx's treatment of these problems are crucial for his rent theory.

In Marx's theory, there is a systematic tendency for individual values to diverge within sectors of a developed capitalism according to the size distribution of capitals employed. The larger the capital employed the greater the productivity. At the same time, competition coerces individual capitalists to accumulate in order to achieve at least minimum standards of productivity. The result is the establishment of an average or normal size of capital within each sector which sets the market value. The normal capital tends to increase over time, as the market value falls, since individual capitalists seek surplus profits by exceeding the normal capital or attempt to restore profitability by catching up with it. Competition within a sector establishes different levels of profitability according to the sizes of capital advanced. This is something which is characteristic of capitalist production in general and which cannot be confined to the agricultural sector, as if land alone were the source of productivity differences and rent the means of profit equalization. In all sectors, productivity and profitability differences coexist and so they should in agriculture also. Rent should not be seen in terms of taking away those differences in profitability. Rather landed property should be seen as modifying the way in which the differences are formed.

When unequal capitals are applied to the land in Marx's theory, they cannot be treated as extra applications of capital to form an intensive margin. The individual capitalist seeks higher profitability for the application of a larger capital as a whole. However, the surplus profits so created do not necessarily accrue to the capitalist. Rent may be raised as a condition of the larger capital's access to the land and the capitalist will have to share the surplus profits with the landlord. In Ricardo's theory, the result of intensive application of capital is to raise rents so that profitability remains equal. In Marx's theory, rents have the effect of reducing the extent to which surplus profits to capitalists differ. The result is to obstruct intensive capital accumulation on the land since the surplus profits accruing to capitalists in industry in correspondence with their size of capital are in part intercepted and appropriated by landlords in the form of rent as a condition of the application of capital to the land. This appropriation of surplus profits, Marx termed differential rent of the second type, DRII.

In Ricardo's theory, the result of intensive application of capital to the land still leaves rents determined technically, by the last capital rather than the last land in use. This could be the outcome in Marx's theory, but it would be a special case, one for which the normal size of capital has remained unchanged. More generally, landed property will obstruct the increase in the size of normal capital but not absolutely. Consequently, the value of corn will be determined by the productivity of this normal capital which may or may not exhibit diminishing returns as in Ricardo's theory.

Landed property has the effect of appropriating surplus profits in the form of DRII, holding down the increase in the size of normal capital, but existing rents are themselves subject to erosion by the increasing size of normal capital. Differential rents then cannot be determined technically or even exactly within the theory. For, at this level of analysis, the principles underlying the formation of differential rent may have been identified but quantitative determination will depend upon the exact relationship between capital and landed property.

Marx's theory of differential rent is based upon an analysis of the formation of market value and surplus profit through competition within the agricultural sector, under conditions in which landed property intervenes in the access of capital to the land. Marx also constructs a theory of absolute rent AR and this is based on the intervention that landed property makes on competition between sectors, on the flow of capital to equalize the rate of profit. Differential rent depends upon the production of surplus profits within the agricultural sector which may be appropriated as rent. AR depends upon the production of surplus value within the sector as a whole and is retained there as a rent rather than entering the pool of aggregate surplus value to be redistributed in the formation of the rate of profit.

AR depends upon the flow of capital onto new lands. The flow of capital into agriculture is obstructed by the existence of landed property. If this flow of capital is located on existing lands in use then the principles of differential rent would apply. But if the use of new lands alone is taken to be the cause of AR, then it will appear simply as a monopoly rent, a forcing up of the market price of corn. This would occur quite independently of the flow of capital onto new lands. It depends upon whether a monopoly can be established in the supply of corn rather than in the ownership of land. In addition, Marx's theory of AR requires a lower composition of capital in agriculture than in industry, a condition which is totally arbitrary in the context of such a monopoly.

In purely technical terms, Marx's theory of AR appears as follows. When agriculture has a lower composition of capital than industry, it produces additional surplus value per unit of capital advanced because of the higher proportion of living labour employed. Consequently, in the absence of landed property, its price of production would lie below its value as the proportionately larger quantity of surplus value is in part redistributed to other capitals. However, the effect of landed property is to intervene and prevent the formation of price of production in agriculture. Agricultural commodities sell at a price above price of production but at most at their value, the difference from price of production making up AR which forms an addition to price. Also, the conditions under which AR would disappear are first, if the composition of capital in agriculture is equal to or higher than the average; second, if all land has been taken into cultivation (i.e. AR depends upon the movement onto new land); or third, if the level of development of agriculture equals that of industry.

If our interpretation of Marx's theory of AR is restricted to these technical considerations alone, then it remains a static theory of surplus value distribution and an arbitrary one both in its results and in its conditions for the existence of AR. Why should AR depend upon a low composition of capital and where other industries have a low composition, why should rent not be formed there? Why should AR be limited to the difference between value and price of production and not be forced up?

Marx's theory of AR is not a static theory. It is the pace of development of agriculture relative to industry that is important. When capital flows into a sector, accumulation can take two forms. The existing methods of production can be reproduced so that there is a quantitative expansion of the sector, the composition of capital remaining the same. Alternatively, accumulation can take the form of an introduction of machinery, a relative displacement of living labour and the working up of more raw materials per unit of that labour. Here then, there would be an intensive accumulation of capital, one which would increase the mass of raw materials and other physical means of production per unit of living labour, an increase in the technical composition of capital or TCC. Now the composition of capital in an industry in value terms is made up of two factors, the progress in the TCC and the value of the elements that compose the TCC. To distinguish the developments in the TCC from changes in values Marx terms the first the organic composition of capital OCC and labelled the overall change in the composition the value composition of capital VCC. Of course, for the economy as a whole changes in the OCC are the basis for productivity increases and reduction in values.

When capital flows into agriculture, it too can either be accumulated intensively or extensively. In the first case, it is confronted by landed property with the demand for the payment of DRII. This corresponds to the surplus profits that can be produced by the increasing OCC induced by the intensive accumulation. Alternatively, capital can flow onto new lands without increasing the OCC, but a rent payment will still be demanded as a condition of access to the land. It is necessarily limited by the maximum payment that would accrue in the form of DRII. The difference is that in the one case intensive cultivation has taken place and produces a surplus profit for the individual capital that may be appropriated as DRII, whereas in the second case a rising OCC has been obstructed so that there is an additional production of surplus value in the sector as a whole. This may be appropriated as AR rather than being redistributed in the formation of the rate of profit and prices of production.

These results can be presented more formally. Suppose initially that the OCC is equal across all industries and that the OCC in industry and potentially in agriculture can be increased by a proportion $b > 1$. If c is the value of raw materials worked up by living labour v, then bc can now be worked up. If for the sake of simplicity, we assume that commodities exchange at their values then the rate of profit becomes $r = \dfrac{ev}{bc + v}$ where e is the rate of exploitation, so that ev is the surplus value produced and bc + v is capital advanced. In agriculture, to the extent that intensive cultivation is obstructed, c remains the quantity of value worked up by v. The value of corn remains c + v + ev. Its difference from price of production is:

$$c + v + ev - (c + v)(1 + r)$$

$$= ev - (c + v)r$$

$$= ev - \frac{(c + v)ev}{bc + v}$$

$$= \frac{ev}{bc + v}(bc + v - c - v)$$

$$= rc(b - 1)$$

But rc(b − 1) is precisely the surplus profits arising out of the increase that could occur in the OCC in agriculture since it is the rate of profit multiplied by the additional capital set in motion for intensive cultivation. These surplus profits correspond to the maximum that could be charged as DRII on existing lands and so cannot be exceeded if accumulation takes the form of extensive cultivation.

Marx's theory of AR has to be examined with some care. The conditions for the existence and upper limits of AR may appear arbitrary but only if his theory is considered in a static context. The limits of AR are determined by the surplus profits arising from capital accumulation and changing values. The necessity for AR of a lower OCC in agriculture is an expression of the obstacles to the development of that sector in a dynamic context and is synonymous with a low pace of development relative to industry, rather than a low comparative level of the VCC which may reflect all sorts of natural and technical differences. In short, for Marx's theory of agricultural rent, we see that it is again the specific circumstances in which capital has access to the land that is important rather than the technical conditions of production as such.

This is the point at which we began the presentation of Marx's theory of agricultural rent in this section. There is no general theory of rent for Marx, because of the necessity of incorporating specific historical elements that embody an understanding of the nature of landed property under consideration. Nevertheless Marx's analysis does remain at an abstract level, that is, it does not consider the specific process of rent formation and its effects for a particular country at a particular point in time. Rather than such an examination of what is termed a social formation within Marxist terminology, Marx confronts the tendential laws of capital accumulation with the intervention of a system of landed property and considers the potential effects. Their actual historical occurrence would depend upon a more concrete historical approach, examining exactly how the system of landed property has been formed and is integrated into the circulation of capital as a whole. What exactly are the 'laws' governing the access of capital to the land and how do they interact with the economy?

It is this approach of Marx's which necessarily distances his analysis from those which see rent formation as independent of the system of landowner-ship. For these, the abolition of private ownership of land and its being taken into state ownership merely diverts the rents from landlords to the state. This can, however, only be asserted because the role of private owner-ship has not been examined, let alone understood, and the system of access to the land under state ownership has not been specified. This follows from the reduction of the process and effects of rent formation to the prevailing natural conditions of fertility and location. Once this is done, it is hardly surprising that changes in the *system* of landownership become seen simply as a change in the *recipients* of rents (within a theory which is itself independent of the system of landownership).

Marx's own comments on state ownership of land are few and scattered but they are sufficient to demonstrate his differences from other writers. He emphasizes that there must be some system of production, whether private or state, which excludes land from being the common property of the people. For otherwise, wage-earners would have an independent source of livelihood and would not be compelled to sell their labour power as a commodity. For the capitalist mode of production, 'its only require-ment is that land should *not* be common property, that it should confront the working class as a condition of production, *not belonging* to it, and the purpose is completely fulfilled if it becomes state property, i.e. if the state draws the rent' (*Theories of Surplus Value*, Part II (TSV II), p. 44). As a result, the landowners as such are superfluous, whatever their importance in the Middle Ages, and the industrialists as a whole have their interests represented by the state appropriating land as their common property as a means of reducing taxes:

Capital cannot abolish landed property. But by converting it into rent (which is paid to the State) the capitalists as a *class* appropriate it and use it to defray their state expenses, thus appropriating it in a roundabout way that cannot be retained directly (TSV III, p. 472, see also continuation of quotation above).

Marx is, however, more or less silent on the levels of rents and prices for state ownership of land, observing that rent as such would remain (TSV II, p. 103/4), possibly at the same level 'if everything else being equal' (*Capital III*, p. 661). He does note, however, the policy implications of the Ricardian theory, that rent is the most satisfactory source of taxation since this would leave prices unchanged. Here there is a parallel with the Physiocratic theory which *contra* Ricardo saw agricultural labour alone as productive of surplus value. For them, despite or because of their identification of surplus value production with the land, taxes must fall upon agriculture. They do so most efficiently when directly applied so that industrial production, parasitic on agriculture though it is, can prosper unimpeded (TSV I, p. 52/3). Nevertheless, despite such motivation and theoretical support, the bourgeoisie hesitate before appropriating landed property:

The radical bourgeoisie (with an eye moreover to the suppression of all other taxes) therefore goes forward theoretically to a refutation of the private ownership of land, which, in the form of state property, he would like to turn into the common property of the bourgeois class, of capital. But in practice he lacks the courage, since an attack on one form of property – a form of the private ownership of a condition of labour – might cast considerable doubts on the other form. Besides, the bourgeois has himself become an owner of land (TSV II, p. 42/3).

If the abolition of private property in land occurs, Marx does admit that the obstacles to capitalist investment might be removed. But this must be interpreted with caution as we have already seen that landed property as such cannot be abolished by capital. What Marx presumably has in mind is that the specificity of agricultural production in relation to other industries is no longer to be located in terms of a special connection with landed property. After all, production in general does take place on land for every sector:

If we consider the cases in a country with capitalist production, where the investment of capital in the land can take place without payment of rent, we shall find that they are all based on a *de facto* abolition of landed property, if not also the legal abolition; this, however, can only take place under very specific circumstances which are by their very nature accidental (*Capital III*, p. 751).

Further Reading

Again, there is no substitute for reading Chapter II of his *Principles* in order to understand Ricardo's theory of rent. Marx's theory is very poorly laid out, in unfinished form, in Volume III of *Capital* together with his criticisms of other writers in Part II of *Theories of Surplus Value*. I have tried to interpret his contribution at greater length in 'On Marx's Theory of Agricultural Rent' *Economy and Society* (1979). This can be read in conjunction with the debate over that article in the same journal in August 1980. Elsewhere, I have tried to examine the role played by landed property in the development of the British coal industry; see particularly 'Royalty or Rent: What's in a Name?' *Birkbeck Discussion Paper*, No. 91, (1981).

5
Smith's Value Theory

The Origins of Smith's Value Theory

Smith's consideration of value begins with the rude society where the hunters of deer and beaver exchange their products according to the labour time taken in the respective chases. Different labours may count unequally as they embody more or less skill, danger and inconvenience. Smith, in *The Wealth of Nations*, opens Chapter VI of Book I entitled 'Of the Component Parts of the Price of Commodities' as follows:

In that early and rude state of society which precedes both the accumulation of stock and the appropriation of land, the proportion between the quantities of labour necessary for acquiring different objects seems to be the only circumstance which can afford any rule for exchanging them one for another.

He goes on to qualify this statement for different degrees of hardship, dexterity and ingenuity.

Here there is no question of 'component parts' intervening to form price. Once, however, a stock means of production and subsistence is accumulated, the product of labour no longer remains exclusively in the hands of the labourer. The owner of the stock will expect a return so that net product will be divided between what might be interpreted to be wages and profits (even if exchange let alone wage-labour is an anachronism for the rude society). This very division leads Smith to reject a theory of exchange value based on labour time. It is a rejection which is reinforced by the observation that 'as soon as the land of any country has all become private property, the landlords, like all other men, love to reap where they have never sowed, and demand a rent even for its natural produce' (p. 152). Thus, rent becomes an additional component of price and drives a further wedge between exchange value and relative labour-time. Nevertheless, Smith remains sympathetic to the idea that labour is both a source and measure of value, but confusingly mixes notions of labour commanded (the amount of labour that can be employed) with the labour expended:

The real value of all the different component parts of price, it must be observed, is measured by the quantity of labour which they can, each of them, purchase or command. Labour measures the value not only of that part of price which resolves itself into labour, but of that which resolves itself into rent, and of that which resolves itself into profit.

But the unmistakeable conclusion is that prices are made up of the three constituent parts that form wages, profits and rents:

In every society the price of every commodity finally resolves itself into some one or other, or all of these three parts; and in every improved society, all the three enter more or less, as component parts, into the price of the far greater part of commodities (p. 153).

It is, of course, Ricardo's criticism of Smith that the division between wages and profits does not necessarily lead to a divergence between value and exchange value, although Ricardo must admit this divergence once commodities are produced with differing ratios of fixed and circulating capital (see chapter 2). For the moment, we can observe that Smith's rejection of a value theory based on labour-time contains the following elements: a comparison of the rude with commercial society by the introduction of a division between wages and profits (this itself is linked to the accumulation of a stock) and the development of private property in land.

A further element in Smith's theory of value is provided by his attempt to measure value by some invariant standard. At times he falls back upon the measure provided by labour-time, as this represents the toil and trouble of acquiring a product. He is more keenly attracted, however, to the notion of labour commanded. By this is meant that each commodity should be measured against the quantity of labour that can be employed by it. If, for the sake of argument, commodities are exchanging at their values, then labour commanded as a measure of value would uniformly differ from labour-time itself in proportion to the level of wages. More generally, the measure of labour commanded simply deflates the price of every commodity by the wage level.

The invariant standard or measure of value is not put forward then in order to explain exchange value. It has a different purpose. Smith is attempting to measure the extent to which surplus labour can be employed in the economy. Here perhaps, he is heavily influenced by Physiocratic theory for which the agricultural surplus measured in physical terms is the means by which unproductive retainers and manufacturers are maintained. Not surprisingly, Smith focuses on corn as the best measure of value in this context since, being a major component in subsistence, it commands labour most uniformly over the centuries. Smith does, however, reject the Physiocratic view that agricultural labour is the sole source of surplus value. Nevertheless, his commitment to an invariant standard of value measured by labour commanded demonstrates the introduction of an understanding drawn from the agricultural stage of society into his theory of value. This is important for his theory of rent, as we shall see later in this chapter and, in more detail, in chapter 6.

Smith does not replace a labour theory of value by a labour commanded theory. The latter serves merely as a measure of value. Instead Smith develops a theory of value based on the three component parts of wages, profits and rents that make up price. In the first instance, this appears to exclude the component part of price that is formed out of raw materials. However, Smith argues that these raw materials themselves embody wage, profit and rent components and so do the raw materials used to produce the raw materials and so on. Ultimately, the price of any commodity, including its raw material costs, can be resolved into the three constituent components:

> In the price of corn, for example, one part pays the rent of the landlord, another pays the wages or maintenance of the labourers and labouring cattle employed in producing it, and the third pays the profit of the farmer. These three parts seem either immediately or ultimately to make up the whole price of corn. A fourth part, it may perhaps be thought, is necessary for replacing the stock of the farmer, or for compensating the wear and tear of his labouring cattle, and other instruments of husbandry. But it must be considered that the price of any instrument of husbandry, such as a labouring horse, is itself made up of the same three parts . . . the whole price still resolves itself either immediately or ultimately into the same three parts of rent, labour and profit (p. 153).

Here we have a procedure that is similar to the Sraffian reduction of price to dated labour (wage component) discounted to the present by the rate of profit (profit component). There is, however, the added complication of the third component, rent. As it stands, this is not a theory of value since it does not explain how value is formed quantitatively. It is merely a tautologous relation between price and its constituent elements. What Smith does is to proceed to determine the three elements independently of each other. This is to construct a theory of value since price is formed from the sum of independently determined components. But it is a theory that contains a serious error. The sum of the three components is constrained to exhaust the net product exactly. Knowledge of any two leaves the other as a residual. All three cannot be determined independently. This can be put another, by now familiar way. Smith is led by his components theory to the conclusion that an increase in wages increases all prices. For this, he can be devastatingly criticized by Ricardo who shows that wage increases are offset by decreases in the rate of profit (exactly if commodities exchange at their values).

Smith has committed an error and it is important to understand why for otherwise we will fail to comprehend how he sets about determining the three independent component parts of price that are not in fact independent. One source of the error is Smith's tendency to conflate arguments that may hold for an individual sector with arguments for the economy as a whole. The special nature of the capital, labour or land used in the

production of a commodity may raise its price relative to others in correspondence with the higher profit, wage or rent. But this is a higher price at
the expense of the prices of other commodities so that a higher component
in general does not lead to a higher price level in general. Smith's confusion of a sector with the economy as a whole is itself a particular instance of
a more general tendency to identify his own economic thinking with the
consciousness of an individual capitalist in competition. He correctly per-
ceives that price can be resolved into the three component parts but then
he reverses the determination and makes each component part contribute
independently to value. Once wages and rent have been settled, the
individual capitalist demands a normal rate of profit be marked up to form
price. In aggregate, however, that mark-up is restricted by the net product
that has already been ear-marked for wages and rent.

The major source of Smith's confusion is, however, derived from his
intermingling of dynamic and static influences in his value theory. As we
shall see in the following section, it is this that appears to allow him to
determine the three components independently. It is important to understand the distinctiveness of Smith's articulation of dynamics and statics.
For Ricardo, values can change over time because of productivity increase
through the introduction of machinery, for example, or through productivity decline through movement onto worse lands. At each moment of
time, commodities have values which may, nevertheless, be under a process of change. It is as if at any time a snapshot of the economy will allow us
to determine values. In contrast, for Smith, value is determined in part by
the process of change itself. A snapshot of the economy will not be able to
tell us what values should be. Thus, as the economy moves out of the
simplest form of the rude society, the very division of net produce into
wages and profits modifies prices. This is linked to the roles played by the
increasing division of labour and the accumulation of a stock.

There is nothing inconsistent as such in values being determined by a
process of change. Where Smith does become inconsistent is in treating the
role played by the way in which things are changing as if they were independent of the way in which they are. This emerges most clearly in his
exclusion of raw materials from the component part of price, and by taking
account of these through a further reduction to component parts. This pre-
supposes that the component parts are constant through time and so they
cannot be determined independently by variables of change. The reduction of the 'fourth part' to magnitudes related to the *current* values of the
other three parts depends upon unchanging conditions through time. Put
another way, the (value of) raw materials provides a connection between
the present and the future, so that the independent formation and division
of the present net product cannot be projected back into the past to alter
the sum of the components there. This is the source of wages, profits and
rents as independent components of price, and hence of varying net

product. The potential for productivity increase, that forms a part of Smith's theory of the determination of the components, cannot change the production that has already taken place. Consequently, Smith's passage around raw materials is the application of a static theory of value determination and it proves inconsistent with the dynamic elements in his independent determination of the components.

Wages, Profits and Rents

Smith's determination of wages can be quite easily seen to be derived from dynamic elements within his theory. He distinguished three states of society within the commercial stage: the progressive, stationary and stagnant. These reflect, respectively, whether the economy is subject to positive, zero or negative growth rates. The level of wages would only be high for the progressive state of society:

It deserves to be remarked, perhaps, that it is in the progressive state, while the society is advancing to the further acquisition, rather than when it has acquired its full complement of riches, that the conditions of the labouring poor, of the great body of the people, seems to be the happiest and the most comfortable. It is hard in the stationary and miserable in the declining. The progressive state is in reality the cheerful and the hearty state to all the different orders of the society. The stationary is dull; the declining melancholy (p. 184).

Smith's argument for this is based on the supply of and demand for labour. Whilst accumulation is taking place, the supply of labour can be outstripped by the demand for labour. Smith also subscribes to what was to become the Malthusian theory of population growth, that high wages produce an expansion in the labouring population as subsistence levels are exceeded:

The liberal reward of labour, therefore, as it is the effect of increasing wealth, so it is the cause of increasing population. To complain of it is to lament over the necessary effect and cause of the greatest public prosperity (p. 184).

Whether the high wages are maintained or not depends upon the extent to which capital accumulation proceeds faster than population growth. In Smith's theory, this is not only possible but most likely. Whilst 'the liberal reward of labour, therefore, as it encourages the propagation, so it increases the industry of the common people' (p. 184). Accumulation is associated with a quantitative expansion that includes the productivity increases induced by a growing division of labour. The wealth produced is a source of a further accumulation of stock and continues to maintain the high demand for labour even relative to the expanding population. To confirm the relationship that he draws between accumulation, division of labour and the level of wages, Smith concludes that high wages are not associated with a highly developed division of labour but with a *growing* division of labour. Nothing can make clearer the dependence of Smith's theory of wages on dynamic factors:

It is not the actual greatness of national wealth, but its continual increase, which occasions a rise in the wages of labour. It is not, accordingly, in the richest countries, but in the most thriving, or in those which are growing rich the fastest, that the wages of labour are highest. England is certainly, in the present times, a much richer country than any part of North America. The wages of labour, however, are much higher in North America than in any part of England (p. 172).

It remains to explain why high wages are not sustained indefinitely together with the accumulation, division of labour and productivity growth that exceeds the population growth induced by high wages. Here the priority that Smith assigns to the extent of the market in constraining the division of labour is crucial. Ultimately the accumulation exhausts markets, and population growth at the high levels of wages no longer leads to productivity increase as the division of labour is constrained. Demand for labour falls relative to supply and with it the level of wages as the economy moves into the melancholy of the stationary state.

In Smith's theory, profits are regulated by quite different principles than wages, although they also depend upon the state of society. Profits are the natural return to be expected for the advance of a stock. When wages are increasing in the progressive state of society, there is a tendency for profits to decline. Here we have what appears to be a Ricardian argument that does not allow wages and profits to be components determined independently of each other. Smith opens Chapter IX, 'Of the Profits of Stock' as follows:

The rise and fall in the profits of stock depend upon the same causes with the rise and fall in the wages of labour, the increasing or declining state of the wealth of the society but those causes affect the one and the other very differently. The increase of stock, which raises wages, tends to lower profits.

This is, however, only a tendency since Smith has already associated the rising wages themselves with increasing division of labour and productivity so that profits can increase along with wages. It all depends upon the extent to which accumulation has exhausted the market. It is here that Smith places primary emphasis, continuing from above:

When the stocks of many rich merchants are turned into the same trade their mutual competition naturally tends to lower its profit; and when there is a like increase of stock in all the different trades carried on in the same society, the same competition must produce the same effect in them all.

Consequently, Smith's theory of profits is drawn from both static and dynamic factors. There is a static distributional conflict between wages and profits, but a dynamic expansion of both through a growing division of labour, if allowed by an unconstrained market.

Smith's arguments are not perhaps as clearly stated by himself as they have been presented here. This is because of his combining together a number of elements some of which are compatible with each other, whilst others are not. He does carry Ricardian elements of conflict between the level of wages and profits, even though the expanding division of labour can expand both. This expansion is itself limited by the extent of the market but is often argued for, by comparison between one particular sector and the economy as a whole. For example, at times, he argues that an extension of demand in a sector increases the price initially but stimulates an increased division of labour which will reduce the price below its former level. Similarly, increased wages lead to higher prices in general, but they are themselves caused by factors which promote the division of labour and reduce prices.

By sector or for the whole economy then, prices decline as the division of labour develops in the progressive state. Now for a single sector, an increase in the capital supplied will stretch the market to its limits, exhaust the opportunities for the division of labour, and confront a decreasing price. The conclusion is drawn by Smith, however, for the economy as a whole in the form that the less the stock of capital the higher the prices and profits as capital is more scarce relative to market constrained opportunities to exploit a division of labour (p. 196). He ignores, as accumulation takes place as a whole, that prices of inputs are decreased for capitalists because he mistakes the role played by raw materials in price formation, a confusion we have already observed in the previous section. For the economy as a whole, profits and markets are expanded for each sector, even if a particular sector cannot expand these on its own.

Smith's theory of rent has been criticized time and time again for inconsistency. We examine it in more detail in chapter 7. Here we are concerned more with its relation to value theory. He himself first observes that as a component part of price, rent is determined by principles that differ from those applying to wages and profits. High or low wages and profits are the cause of high or low price, whereas rent is the effect of it. If Smith intended this alone to be his theory of rent, then he would have been anticipating the Ricardian theory of rent, if not value, and it is difficult to see how rent could enter as a component part of price. However, he goes onto divide commodities produced on the land into two types, those that always afford a rent and those that only do sometimes. Thus, whether there is rent at all or not depends upon the product and not upon the price. Once he has decided that a product always bears a rent then he can determine whether it is high or low according to the product's price. But there is always some irreducible element of rent that enters as a component part of price. This is inconsistent with the Ricardian theory, for which there is a no rent land on the extensive (or, if necessary, intensive) margin.

To observe that Smith maintains that there is an absolute portion of rent that always enters as a component part of price is not to explain why he should believe this. His explanation is based on the incorporation of Physiocratic notions into his theory. For the Physiocrats, agriculture is the sole source of a (physical) surplus which in the form of rent maintains unproductive retainers and manufacturers. We have already seen how Smith appears to draw upon these notions to suggest a measure of value by labour commanded. The quantity of labour commanded will be determined by the ratio of absolute fertility to the level of subsistence. It is this which provides Smith with his causative rent component of price. It is subsistence goods which always afford a rent. They do so because land will deliver up a higher level of output than is necessary to maintain labour, and landlords will demand a portion of that surplus as a consequence of their ownership of land. Smith even goes into the details of the different shares of rents that would prevail according to what constitutes the subsistence commodity. For a rice producing country, rents will be much higher than for one relying upon corn, because, after paying subsistence, an average rice field leaves a greater surplus than even the most fertile corn field.

For Ricardian theory, Smith's absolute component of rent would be eroded by competition from land that otherwise lies uncultivated. Differential rent alone can exist. The two determine rent according to different principles, even if both conclude that rent increases with the progress of society. Differential rents increase for Ricardo as the extensive and intensive margins are stretched. These are complemented in Smith's theory by the absolute rents that accrue with fertility and surplus increase, together with the rents that accrue from products that previously afforded none when the demand was lower for them in a less wealthy economy. Ricardo's rents are determined independently of the system of landed property: they are a technical product of differential products appropriated by whoever happens to own the better land. In Smith's analysis, the obstacle that landed property poses to capital is theorized by the incorporation of Physiocratic notions. Smith insists that a rent must be paid for the use by another of a land in private ownership. The absolute fertility of land relative to subsistence as a source of an absolute rent is the proxy that Smith uses to stand for the intervention of landed property.

Competition in Smith and Ricardo

We shall not be concerned in this section with the extent to which the different risks, skills and agreeablenesses of the various occupations for land, capital and labour lead to differentials in the levels of rents, profits and wages. We will examine how competition exists in Smith's theory as a result of the way in which prices are formed and contrast it with Ricardo's theory. In the previous section, we have seen that the components theory determines the elements of wages, profits and rents independently by a combination of dynamic and static factors associated with the level and the rate of increase of the division of labour. One important result of the components theory is that the Ricardian problem of the divergence between value and exchange value does not have to be faced, since value itself has been rejected as the independent source of exchange value. This is not a result of Smith's reaction to the divergence between value and exchange value when compositions of capital differ. It is a reaction to the division between wages and profits that occurs when a stock is accumulated to promote the division of labour quite independently of the uniformity of compositions across sectors for that original division of labour. Ricardo can show that Smith is wrong. The division between wages and profits does not of itself violate the exchange of commodities at their value. But, in showing that Smith is wrong, Ricardo demonstrates the inadequacies of his own theory. Value and exchange value cannot be identified with each other even if Smith says they cannot for the wrong reason. In terms of competition, Smith is consistent and Ricardo is not. Smith remains at the most complex level of competition for which prices are determined for the individual capitalist by independent components, a theory that reflects the revenue seeking activity of each individual agent. Ricardo hops between competition of capital and labour over the level of wages and profits and competition between capitals to equalize the rate of profit.

Ricardo, however, has the consistency in theorizing competition at the level in which it brings divergence between market and natural price, when supply and demand are unequal. Because his theory of value is based upon the conditions of production, and where necessary, the distributional relations between capital and labour, Ricardo has a theory of natural price which is independent of the forces of supply and demand. The same is not true for Smith. Prices most clearly depend upon the extent of the market or demand and extent and pace of growth of the division of labour or supply. Each component is determined independently according to the supply of and demand for the factor employed. In Smith's theory there can at best be drawn a dividing line between what are considered the natural determinants of supply and demand and what are to be assigned a lower priority as the source of deviations in the market from the natural price.

These differences in the notions of competition in Smith and Ricardo lead to further differences in the manner in which they analyse the movement from market to natural price. For Ricardo, the dynamic element restoring equilibrium is the flow of capital between sectors to equalize the rate of profit. For Smith, if a commodity's market price falls below its natural price, then one of the component parts must be below its natural value. Whichever one it is will be withdrawn and price will be restored to its natural level. But Smith forgets that the factor has remained unemployed. Wherever it is reinserted into the economy, it will be paid below its natural level and reduce market price below natural price. Smith's error lies in determining the components independently. A price reduction in one sector is an increase in the market value of one or more components at the expense of the other or others, as Ricardo points out in his criticism of Smith. It is an error that has an added significance in treating the components symmetrically as market prices fluctuate around natural prices. It is as if each factor of production is equally mobile and occupies an equal position in the reorganization of production, whereas it is capital that flows between sectors for this purpose in Ricardo's theory, and which is the dominating power of reorganizing the economy in capitalist society.

Further Reading

Chapters V-XI of Book One of the *The Wealth of Nations* are strongly recommended although they are full of digressions. In *Theories of Surplus Value*, Part II, Marx dissects the value theories of Smith and Ricardo, but the material is not systematically organized.

6
The Marginalist Revolution and Neo-classical Economics

The Elements of Neo-classical Economics

Anybody reading a modern textbook of economics and then a work of classical political economy cannot fail but to be struck by the contrast in the problems posed and the methods of solution and analysis used. It is generally recognized that around the 1870s the marginalist revolution in economic thought represented a sharp break with the theory of the past and launched the modern orthodoxy that has subsequently been perfected and developed but rarely challenged. Even the Keynesian revolution leaves intact the principles associated with marginalism and merely serves to raise the question of the relationship between individual and aggregate economic behaviour, between micro- and macro- economics. A reading of an economics text of the 1870s or thereabouts would still reveal sharp contrasts with the classics but the contrasts are imperfect and contain elements of continuity with the past. We will go some way to explaining this later on. For the moment we are more concerned with the contrasts in a more perfect form.

One of the most striking features of modern economic theory is its method of building models. A look through any journal of economic theory will reveal an exposition of these models of the economy more than an attempt to theorize the economy itself. Model-building has become so well-established that debates can concern the properties of the different models rather than a direct debate over an explanation of economic reality. It is as if architects took it upon themselves to debate the merits of their drawings and blueprints rather than the buildings that they are supposed to represent. Of course, this characteristic of modern economic theory has not gone unnoticed. The theory is criticized as being unrealistic and dictated to by the demands of the model-building rather than by the demands of realism. The architect does not plan for two-dimensional buildings because of the paper limitations upon three-dimensional drawings. But the modern economist does tend to constrain and determine his models by the limitations of the techniques available to him. If the model becomes a mess without certain assumptions, then those assumptions must be made and both the real world and realism must be sacrificed. This is most clear in the assumptions that are made for the existence of an equilibrium, assumptions which violate the simplest experiences of the real world: that there should, for example, be diminishing returns to scale.

To criticize modern economic theory for its lack of realism is a telling but limited commentary. It suggests that one set of realistic assumptions should replace a set of unrealistic ones. The problem is rather that abstraction within the theory has taken the distorted form of making assumptions and this cannot be corrected simply by changing the assumptions. No distinctions are drawn between the status of concepts in terms of some explaining and underlying the existence of others. In addition, the appeal to realism to justify these assumptions depends upon an externally predetermined notion of what constitutes the facts of realism. Whether the facts of reality are used to validate the assumptions initially or in conclusion by statistical verification of predictions, this notion of realism is problematic. We have discussed this at some length in the first chapter and we emphasize again that this is a specific way in which modern economics incorporates empirical material into its theory, by leaving the material at the margins of the theory as its starting point for more or less realistic assumptions or its closing point for verifying predictions.

This method of utilizing empirical material at the margins contrasts with classical political economy and is not unrelated to the narrowing of the scope of economic theory. With Marshall, political economy became that branch of the object which applied economic principles to political questions. For the classics, political economy was the study of the economy within society, so that there could be no separation of 'the principles' from their social and political context. This is most noticeable in the significance of class relations for the classics whereas these become at most identified with the provision of factor inputs in modern economics.

With the development of economics itself, principally as a response to the rise of capitalism, understandings of society tended to isolate the economy from the rest of society as a separated object of study. This conforms with the apparent organization of capitalism itself, as if the economy could be understood in isolation from the political, legal and other necessary conditions for its existence. This is characteristic of classical political economy, clearly for Ricardo, for example, more so than for Smith but the use of an analysis based on class relations retained however indirect a link with the more general conditions within society. For Marx, who also makes an analysis of capital as economic reproduction, the connection between economy and society is ensured through the notion of mode of production, for which there are necessary relations between economic and non-economic factors. But for neo-classical economics, the separation between economy and society is perfected, particularly by the extent to which economic relations are reduced to technical ones, most noticeably in mathematical form, and from which other considerations can be excluded. What is proudly pronounced to be the separation of positive from normative economics, the verifiable from the judgemental, is perhaps more significantly the separation of economic analysis from its satisfactory location within society, except as an 'afterthought' to come to a practical decision. Nevertheless modern economics does incorporate empirical material into its analysis simply by the variables it chooses to examine. To study the relationship between wages, prices and profits, for example, is to recognize, however unconsciously, that capitalism is under scrutiny and this does delimit the scope of the analysis accordingly. Yet neo-classical economics proceeds to explain these historically delimited categories by ahistorical theorizing, by the use of concepts and relations that would apply in all societies. Whilst supply and demand interacting through price relations is specific to a market economy, the explanation of each is not. The theory of the ability to supply is based on unexplained technical relations between inputs and outputs, relations that exist in all societies. Demand is derived from exogenously determined preferences which are also not specific to the market or capitalist economy. But if prices, wages, profits or whatever are ultimately explained by concepts which correspond to societies in which these categories do not exist then the explanation must be wrong for otherwise prices, wages and so on would exist in all these societies.

There is, however, an escape route. The theory only pertains to societies in which certain 'institutional' conditions are present such as the market. This has the unfortunate consequence of locating the explanatory factors of the theory externally, unexamined, something which is recognized by economics in delegating the task to other disciplines such as history or sociology. So general equilibrium theory takes as given the initial endowment of individuals, their preferences and the technology with which they can produce. The resulting equilibrium can be seen to be caused by these exogenous factors: it would change as they do. The causative factors are themselves unexamined and this is equally true of the economic, as social relations that bind the individual economic units together.

As we observed in the first chapter, there is an inconsistency in neo-classical economics at the conceptual level and this is the source of a causal structure within the theory. Whilst historically specific and social categories are utilized within the theory, they are conflated with the individualized relations out of which they are aggregated. Where uniformities as in prices, for example, or aggregate variables such as employment are assumed to exist then they constrain or have a causal relation to the individual acts of exchange to which they correspond. The logic of the school of thought is to push for an increasing focus upon individual acts of exchange and to define social relations simply in terms of aggregated individual behaviour. Here the contrast exists with the classics' preoccupation with class relations. Where these enter neo-classical economics, they are treated as if they were an average or representative individual in the supply of some factor such as capital, labour or land.

The preoccupation with individual economic behaviour forces neo-classical economics to concern itself with individual motivation. Ultimately this rests upon the notion of exogenously given preferences over consumption goods for each individual whose increasing satisfaction gives rise to increasing utility for the individual. For those engaged in production or supply and not directly in exchange activity for consumption, then profit maximization becomes the goal. This leads to an analysis based on the relation between marginal products of factor inputs and their prices and the marginal utility of consumption goods and their prices. The theory becomes concerned with optimization whether in minimizing the costs of producing a given output or in maximizing profits or in maximizing utility of consumption subject to prices and an income constraint. These concerns conform both to the methods and the limits of the new economics and very much reinforce the use of model-building through the use of mathematics. The application of calculus as the technique of optimization leads to the notion of the margin defined in terms of infinitesimally small increases. The pervasive presence of optimization and hence of marginal utilities and products is what determined that the transition to the modern economics should be termed the marginalist revolution.

But despite the fact that it is called the marginalist revolution and despite the undeniable influence that the margin holds over neo-classical economics, it should not be taken for granted that it is the margin as such which constitutes the break between classical and neo-classical economics. For one thing, the margin is to be found in Ricardian rent theory even if a dose of capital represents the increment rather than an infinitesimally small magnitude. For another, the optimization associated with neo-classical economics does not have to be based upon the techniques associated with calculus but can utilize more general methods involving convexity. If it is not the margin as such which constitutes the basis for the marginalist revolution, it is the *comparison* of margins. What this allows is an analysis of substitution between economic goods, whether as factor inputs in production or as outputs in consumption. The composition of capital and labour, for example, with which production is to take place can be examined. This reflects a change in the problems posed between classical and neo-classical economics.

For the classics, the difference between compositions of capitals between sectors posed the problem of the effects of this on price and profit according to capital advanced. For neo-classical economics the different compositions of capitals within a sector, indeed for individual capitalists, becomes a matter of choice, not of effects. This reflects a change in focus between the two schools, the classics being concerned with the conditions which make accumulation possible at all, whereas the neo-classicals are preoccupied with the conditions that make it most efficiently organized. Perhaps a major stimulus behind this change of focus is the increasing use of machinery as a substitute for labour in the production process during the course of the nineteenth century. The choice between more or less machinery had to be theorized.

If the introduction of machinery can explain the significance of substitution for neo-classical economics, it does not immediately suggest why a theoretical element motivated by production or supply should be carried over into demand in the form of the substitution between consumption goods motivated by the satisfaction of utility. That it does is explained by the neo-classical focus upon individual behaviour and a change from the preoccupation with the conditions necessary for profitable accumulation to the satisfaction that can be provided by the optimal organization of the economy. Significantly, the question of growth in economic theory played a limited role from the demise of classical political economy until the end of the 1930s. Then in the light of the Great Depression, Harrod raised the question of growth again but in terms of the level of aggregate demand rather than by reference to the efficient organization of the economy.

The combination of these elements of neo-classical economics has a number of overall effects and these again can be brought out by contrast to classical theory. Most striking is the transformation in the concept of value. The classics sought an objective basis for value, most notably in the form of the labour theory of value, and, where this failed, in the notion of natural price according to the conditions of production and the time for which capital is advanced. Neo-classical economics identifies value subjectively with the satisfaction that can be obtained by individuals through consumption. From initial endowments through intermediate production to final output of consumption goods, there is a chain of evaluation through marginal products and marginal utilities that ultimately rests upon individual and exogenously given preferences. Whilst the value that is attained by each individual is measured by the extent of preference satisfaction, the level is itself determined by the simultaneous relations between marginal possibilities for production and consumption. Consequently, neo-classical economics does draw a distinction between its subjective theory of what value is and the theory of price by which it is determined at the margin. This distinction between value and price is the basis for the need to measure consumer surplus, to construct price indices and to undertake cost-benefit analysis, since the determination of price at the margin does diverge from the overall determination of neo-classical value which cannot be measured directly by prevailing prices.

Classical political economy distinguishes value and price in a totally different way. Value is objectively determined by some notion of cost of production and price differences from value represent the results of market fluctuations. Thus, classical political economy recognized the distinction between value in use and value in exchange, each a property enjoyed by a commodity. But their focus is upon value in exchange rather than upon value in use, as in neo-classical economics with its preoccupation with consumer satisfaction.

Fluctuations in prices are themselves the outcome of competition between individuals in the market place. For neo-classical economics this raises a problem. Value and price are already determined on the basis of the subjective behaviour of individuals, so any divergence from equilibrium prices because of competition cannot introduce that individual behaviour since it is already there. Accordingly, fluctuations around neo-classical equilibrium price requires there to be a counterposing of one set of perfectly competitive conditions with another set of less than perfect conditions, or more generally for one set of competitive conditions to be set against another. This creates an enormous scope for more or less arbitrary theorizing of what is the natural equilibrium price, the normal conditions of competition, as opposed to the divergence from equilibrium which will result from a violation of those normal conditions.

Without an objective theory of value, the determination of what is the normal or equilibrium price and what constitutes divergence from it must correspond to a division of economic behaviour at the individual level between the normal and the abnormal. Generally, of course, what is normal is taken to be the conditions of perfect competition in which all individuals are price-takers and have equal access to markets, finance and technology. Analysis of divergence around this equilibrium requires assumptions to be made about how individuals would behave in disequilibrium. Alternatively, in the attempt to be more 'realistic', the conditions of perfect competition could be abandoned, and then alternative individual behaviour would constitute the basis for the new normal equilibrium and other violations of this would explain fluctuations. We have here a reproduction of a problem to be found in Smith's theory of competition, as discussed in the last chapter. Once value is itself determined by competition (say at the level of individuals) then it becomes impossible to distinguish what constitutes value and what constitutes divergence from value except through a more or less arbitrary division between normal and abnormal conditions of competition. This can all be stated in another way. Once equilibrium is determined by supply and demand, the question is raised of what are the variables upon which these should depend. For partial equilibrium, it is one price; for general equilibrium it is all prices when perfect competition is assumed. But supply and demand do depend upon a host of other factors and these can be included in the functions to redefine equilibrium rather than divergence from it.

The previous discussion makes clear how much neo-classical economics depends upon theoretical organization around the concept of equilibrium. Certainly classical political economy can also be interpreted in this way because of its preoccupation with stationary states. Even so the focus is more on the movement to the state than on the state itself; Smith's limits to the division of labour is an example, as is Ricardo's declining productivity of agriculture. Equilibrium is itself only possible if certain conditions remain fixed and hence, as we have observed earlier, in this and the first chapter, become unexplained and yet causative. There is room for simultaneous determination of endogenous variables, but some exogenous factors must remain. For general equilibrium theory these factors are the initial endowments and preferences of individuals and the technical relations of production. How these do change might be thought to be more important for explaining economic progress than the equilibrium to which they give rise. In addition, the method of attaining equilibrium in conditions of perfect competition requires that all individuals be price-takers. This has the nonsensical implication that all prices are given with nobody to set them unless some fictional (Walrasian) auctioneer is allowed to perform the task.

We have shown that both neo-classical and classical theory draw a distinction between value and price but in ways that profoundly reflect the differences between the theories. The different distinctions also have other implications. For classical theory, the objective determination of value implies that value can be treated independently of the distribution of that value between classes, although this property of the theory is thrown into confusion once the labour theory of value is abandoned. Even then, as the Sraffians demonstrate, distribution can be considered prior to the determination of prices which depend upon the time and rate of interest for which capital is advanced. In contrast, for neo-classical theory, distribution is merely an aspect of price theory. Prices are determined simultaneously and these give rise to revenues which accrue to the owners of initial endowments of factor inputs.

Finally, we observe that neo-classical theory produces another remarkable result, a very limited ability to distinguish between what is production and what is consumption. Formally, within theory, the two are almost identical, even if they can be conceptually distinguished. In pursuit of profit maximization, an entrepreneur will minimize the costs of producing a given level of output. Similarly, an individual minimizes the cost of attaining a given level of utility. It is as if the consumer is engaged in an act of producing welfare at given costs of inputs (consumption goods) and a given technology (preferences). In this way, the consumer is treated like a producer. On the other hand, production is treated as if it is merely the consumption of inputs to produce definite results, in this case outputs rather than immediate gratification. There is no significance attached to the fact that one of the inputs is labour and involves a production process. In this sense, production is treated as though it were identical to consumption. A significant result of this is the reluctance of neo-classical economics to examine the labour process in any other than a formal technical way, as a relationship between inhuman inputs and outputs. Labour is simply 'consumed' in the production process as a means of creating output just as the other inputs are so consumed. Here the absence of the division of labour that preoccupied Smith is notable.

The Marginalist Revolution

The marginalist revolution, which is usually associated with economists such as Jevons and Walras, embodied most of the elements of neo-classical economics that have been described in the previous section. In particular, there was a clear understanding of the notion of general equilibrium, of its ultimate dependence upon individually derived utility and of the determination of prices at the margin. Initially, the full potential for theorizing substitution between goods and simultaneity between markets may not have been realized. But the conceptual apparatus certainly did exist. It is important to emphasize this, for we shall argue later that there was a reaction within the school of marginalism against the full thrust of its implications. It would be easy simply to see this as a hangover from the classics or as a slow process of diffusion of the new ideas. These influences do exist but such a psychological explanation for the history of economic thought is unsatisfactory, for it takes no account of the specific resistance to specific ideas.

One of the major characteristics of the marginalist revolution is the generalization of the margin from agriculture to industry as a whole. Whereas Ricardo appears to be caught between a value theory based on average labour-time for industry and marginal labour-time for agriculture, the marginalists reject the labour theory of value altogether and treat agriculture and industry equally. For each, value is determined at the margin. Thus, Jevons can argue that Ricardo's rent theory is in all respects correct and merely needs to be applied to the economy as a whole at the expense of a value theory based on labour time.

The generalization of the Ricardian theory of rent to the economy as a whole has, however, a paradoxical effect. Whilst the theory of value associated with rent seems to have gained victory in an analytical war, it does so only at the expense of abolishing a distinction between agriculture and industry since each is treated identically. More alarming is that the differential surplus associated with rent is now identified with other factor rewards, such as profits, since these are the form that the surplus is presumed to take for industry in general. In other words, the generalization of rent theory to the economy as a whole has the effect of dissolving the specifity of a theory of rent itself. One cannot help but be reminded of the conquering imperialist power losing itself in the culture of its colony!

It could be argued, and it sometimes is, that the loss of a specific rent theory is a virtue. In parallel with this, all assets even such as labour itself, become a form of wealth and hence capital. This is most clear in the theory of human capital. In this way categories such as wages, profits and rents become seen as accidental, historical or convenient forms of terminology when they are, from the economic point of view, essentially equivalent: the different prices for different factors. The ideological content of such an approach is unmistakeable. By reducing the role of the classes related to these revenues to one of equivalence it places them in a position of symmetry in which each may exploit the others by an inappropriately high price. The theoretical mechanism for doing so is equality before the market to exchange freely but it is a very blinkered understanding of capitalist society.

The force of classical political economy and of Marx's theory also is that the existence of rent as a category distinct from profit (itself distinct from wages) is symptomatic of a special role played by land and landed property. This should at least be rooted out and understood rather than denied at the outset by 'first principles'. Indeed, as we shall see, the marginalists themselves were initially distinctly uneasy about the implications of these 'first principles' for distribution theory.

For the loss of rent theory or equivalently its rise to dominance is most profoundly felt in the theory of distribution, for which rent determination, as distinct from profit and wage determination, is a part. We observed in the previous section that one result of neo-classical economics is to reduce distribution theory to an accounting deduction from previously determined prices. To some extent this can be concealed if factor inputs are treated in aggregate as capital, labour and land, independently of the individuals who own them and if demand is placed in the background by assuming a single output. Then prices of factor inputs, or distributional relations, are simply determined by the productivity of the factors at the margin, by marginal products. The result is that the principles by which profits, rents and wages are determined are identical. The same conclusion can be drawn in the more general case of substitution between consumption goods. It is a matter of working out the supply of and demand for each factor at a given set of prices, equilibrium being determined by those prices and derived factor incomes for which supply and demand are equalized in every market.

It is important to emphasize that the early marginalists did not treat wages, profits and rents as the same, only that the principles by which they are determined became identical. (Contrast with Ricardo, for whom value in industry and value in agriculture are determined by different principles.) Since the economy is seen by the marginalists as the equilibrium of supply and demand in each and every market, the determination of any factor income is made through an analysis of the supply and demand for that factor. Accordingly, different factor incomes can be distinguished only by examining differences for that factor in the conditions of supply, demand or both. This is the only way the early marginalists can distinguish between capital, labour and land and their associated revenues, profits, wages and rent.

Consider land, for example. As a factor input, used in production, it is like any other input from the point of view of the capitalist. It is to be assessed for its productivity as set against its cost, in this case rent. As a result, the demand for land is not special as compared with other inputs. However, on the supply side, land is uniquely defined for the marginalists by its being supposedly fixed in supply. It has a particularly unique price-inelastic supply curve, as indeed would any other natural resource. Labour is also not treated as a special input in any way from the perspective of the capitalist. On the supply side, each labourer has a fixed endowment of hours to divide between work and leisure. The one is associated with disutility and the other with positive utility. Consequently, the supply of labour is uniquely determined by the individual choices made by workers between the utility and disutility of leisure and work.

Finally, capital can be defined in two respects. It is not fixed in supply, once time is taken into account. Indeed, capital is treated in terms of the productivity of time, although this can be more or less directly done. A tree left to grow will produce more timber than one felled immediately, so that a growing tree represents capital. This is the notion of capital associated with what came to be called the Austrian School. The time taken to produce a tool to aid production may delay but will increase the output created. The more roundabout or time-consuming the production process the more the output that can be produced. The most significant indicator of capital is not simply the passage of time as in the case of the tree, but rather the embodiment of that time in physical means of production. This is where we get our notion of capital as machines and from which can be calculated marginal products. This is the more familiar form in which we meet the notion of capital in modern economics.

It is, however, conceptually supported by the Austrian notion of productivity of time. The *demand* for capital is then determined by the entrepreneur's choice over the productivity of time/machines compared to its cost, namely the rate of interest or profit (the two are treated identically in the absence of money). The *supply* of capital is fluid because of time and depends upon the choice between present and future consumption (more wood tomorrow or less wood today). The more an individual is prepared to abstain from present consumption and to wait for future consumption, the greater is the supply of capital. As it is generally believed that there is a preference for present as opposed to future consumption, the necessary inducement to supply capital is the reward for abstinence or waiting provided through the rate of interest/profit. In short, the rate of profit is determined by the supply of and demand for capital which are themselves associated with the interaction between the preference for present consumption against abstinence and the productivity of time.

Significantly, for each of these specific determinations of factor incomes within the same principles of supply and demand, the explanatory elements are totally ahistorical. Land has always been fixed in supply to the extent that it can ever be said to do so. Work and leisure are mutually exclusive uses of time in any society once the division can be drawn between the two (and it is perhaps for a capitalist society that the distinction is most sharply drawn). The use of produced means of production and their necessary dependence upon abstinence is not unique to capitalism. It must be concluded that wages, profits and rents have not been adequately explained within the theory since they are simply presumed to exist and then merely calculated on the basis of influences that are not sufficient for their existence, for otherwise these revenues would exist in all societies. This remains a valid criticism irrespective of the merits of the method of marginalism by which the factor incomes are calculated.

The reaction against the early marginalists by those who came later, such as Marshall, can perhaps best be seen in this light of limited explanatory power. There developed a distinct uneasiness with the conclusion that wages, profits and rents are to be determined in exactly the same way, a feeling that there is something specific about capital, labour and land and their associated revenues. Those fully embracing the implications of marginalism now began to see distribution as the law of the three rents, each factor input providing a differential surplus between its average and marginal contribution, this in turn being ultimately measured in relation to preference satisfaction. These ideas, however, met a stubborn resistance from those who felt that capital and labour do not constitute land, that rent is specific to land and not to be confused with profit and wages which are specifically associated with the other factors of production. Nor did this obstinacy derive from a wish to cling to the value doctrines of classical political economy. The various elements of the marginalist revolution were more or less universally accepted; it was the implications of these elements that left a residual feeling that something had been lost in the transition between schools of thought. The feeling is well-founded as the specific and distinct principles for determining factor incomes had been eroded. Moreover, it is only during the early days of the revolution in thought, as each economic variable became exposed to theoretical reinterpretation through principles of analytical uniformity, that the loss of what classical political economy had provided could be felt.

Those feeling this sense of bereavement were caught on the horns of a dilemma: how to accept the principles of the marginalist revolution without accepting its implications, the loss of an ability to analyse distinctively factor inputs and their associated revenues. The solution lay in a compromise which involved limiting the principles of marginalism to partial equilibrium analysis. Then rent, for example, could be seen as being derived from a differential surplus in production that accrued to the owners of land as in Ricardian theory. This requires a one-sector economy or for all prices to be fixed other than the one for which land is being used. The same is true for the treatment of capital as a stock of means of production which is fixed in the short run. There it derives a rate of return that is equivalent to a land rent with the exception that over time this rate of return will be modified towards the normal rate of profit as supply of the capital stock is altered.

However, this normal rate of profit is itself left undetermined. Marshall quite eloquently characterized this notion of cac ical by terming its reward a quasi-rent. He recognizes the treatment of capital as if it were a rent, but shrinks from identifying capital with land. So he can neither call the factor payment profit nor rent. Hence the hybrid terminology for a hybrid theory, and it was the hybrid of partial equilibrium analysis that os yructed the development of the new and pure strain of the earliest marginalists that ultimately bred general equilibrium theory.

By comparison with the classics, the marginalists not only felt the peculiar transformation and loss of rent theory but also the introduction of utility theory and the displacement of an objective by a subjective theory of value. Again the change is sharpened for those trained in and familiar with the classical tradition. As a result, it led Jevons to speculate whether utility would subsequently be measured and recorded just as electrical current had been done. Now, with theoretical hindsight, we are aware that demand theory only requires ordinal preferences so that calibration of utility is unnecessary. Nevertheless, Jevons' speculation is indicative of a desire to root the new theory into an objective soil. The same applies to a more sophisticated interpretation of the role that utility plays within the theory. What the market mechanism does is to bring into equivalence the relative marginal utilities of every individual for every good (this argument can be modified to take account of 'corner' solutions). So, there is established on social criteria ratios of marginal utilities to which all the individual ratios correspond. This is perhaps most clear in the case of time preference where the rate of interest expresses the ratio of equivalence socially for each individual between present and future consumption. More generally, Hobson expressed the point very well by arguing that the market mechanism established the worth that a good represents automatically and quite remarkably. How else could we possibly determine the value of a work of art or a particular dwelling?

There is a parallel here between the marginalist theory and Adam Smith's invisible hand, but there are also differences even if Smith's analysis is often viewed as the anticipation of the Pareto-efficiency properties of general equilibrium. Smith's theory concerns the beneficial organization of production at least cost, whereas the marginalists are more concerned with the most beneficial satisfaction of preference. More striking is the parallel between the marginalist argument and the one associated with Marx's theory of value. For the latter, concrete labours are brought into a social equivalence through exchange to create abstract labour as the substance of value. For the marginalist, the welfare of individuals is brought into a social equivalence through an exchange that equates marginal utilities to each other.

From this point, the two theories depart from each other. In Marx's theory, the value relation so established acts as a coercive force on producers within the society and creates a standard to which they must conform, even if the standard is itself subject to change as accumulation yields productivity increase. In this sense the value relation is a social relation around which individuals revolve. The opposite is true for the marginalist theory. The social equivalence is established from the individual propensities and there is no reaction from it back upon them. Changes in the marginal propensities of any individual are exogenous and can have the effect of transforming every equivalence that has been established, even in perverse directions, without any other individual propensity changing at all. In this way, the price relations of the theory merely reflect the bringing into equivalence of individual propensities that are predetermined. We find yet again that social relations can only enter the theory in the form of a parody by which they are fundamentally excluded from being analysed or having any effect.

Further Reading

A reading of the marginalists is most fruitful since they often felt it necessary to bring out and justify their differences with classical political economy. Today the theoretical presumptions of neo-classical economics are concealed but carelessly rather than carefully, 'self-evident' and 'necessary' as they are through the weight of intellectual tradition and through the analytical techniques that are their accompaniment. A. Marshall's *Principles* (1890) are heavy going but Jevons' *The Theory of Political Economy* (1970) is frank and short. The generalization of rent theory to the economy as a whole was made clear by Hobson and Clark independently and considered important enough to justify the publication of both of their contributions in the same issue of the *Quarterly Journal of Economics* in 1891. For a critique of much of modern neo-classical economics see the two books edited by Green and Nore, *Economics: An Anti-Text* and *Issues in Political Economy* (1977 and 1979 respectively).

7
The Euthanasia of Rent Theory

The So-Called Historical Theory of Rent and Price

In the previous chapter we have shown how neo-classical economics represents a break with classical political economy and that it did so by general-
izing rent theory from agriculture to industry, thereby undermining rent
theory itself. At the same time we saw that there was created a certain resistance to the euthanasia of the rent theorist, if not the *rentier*, and that this
was achieved through a preoccupation with partial rather than general
equilibrium. It is not surprising that this resistance should focus on rent
theory since this was most clearly under threat. In this chapter we examine
in more detail the evolution and extinction of rent theory under the rule of
neo-classical economics. In doing so, we will develop in further detail some
of the analysis of the previous chapter and also of chapter 5 and, to a lesser
extent, chapter 4.

The passage to extinction of rent theory in neo-classical economics has
meant that it has lived in the underworld of the profession, like a guilty
conscience that is at its strongest when the crime is committed but which
fades with the passage of time only to re-emerge sporadically and feebly.
But the absence of a rent theory from neo-classical economics is important
and it should not be allowed to pass unnoticed because it helps to demonstrate clearly the character of the theory as a whole.

To some extent our task is made simpler by the existence of a remarkable
article by Buchanan published in 1929. The timing is important. The
debate over rent theory and how it could be accommodated within neo-
classical economics was taking place. The concept of both partial and
general equilibrium were well enough established. In addition, Buchanan
concerned himself with the history of rent theory. Taken together, all these
factors placed Buchanan in a position of attempting to synthesize classical
political economy with two conflicting positions within neo-classical economics, those derived from partial and general equilibrium analysis.

Buchanan sets himself two tasks. First, he states the basis within the
prevailing neo-classical economics for a dispute over whether rent is price
determined or price determining so that he may resolve the conflict

involved. He does so by drawing the distinction between two problems. For one, there is a single product so that the last unit of capital applied pays no rent, determining price and consequently the differential rents on all other units of capital and their associated lands. For the other problem, there are competing demands between products for land usage so that a rent enters into the price of a commodity as the opportunity cost of the land's use for an alternative product. Buchanan prides himself on being the first person to point out 'that the two problems involve different hypotheses and different conclusions.' He could not have searched far for predecessors. Carlton (1906), for example, reviews contemporary debates over rent theory in terms of the use of the margin of transference to alternative land use (marginal rent) as opposed to the extension to inferior lands (differential rent). See also Hollander (1895).

For Buchanan, because rent theory has set itself two different problems he reckons the dispute over rent theory is a false one since 'the essential difference in the two questions is that in one the land was supposed to have an alternative use, while in the other it had none.' Consequently he can close his article with the conclusion that 'The theories . . . are not antagonistic, but complementary; they arise from the application of the same *principle* to *two different questions*, and constitute together something like a complete theory of the subject.' The principle involved for Buchanan is the prevailing marginalist economics, and it is one which was to be applied without differentiation to problems of economic analysis, as we have seen in the previous chapter. But at Buchanan's time of writing there is a tension within this theory between partial and general equilibrium analysis in explaining economic categories. It is a tension which is reproduced in Buchanan's contribution as we shall discuss later.

The second task that Buchanan sets himself is to consider various theories of rent in the light of the two problems he has identified. For him, the history of rent theory is the treatment of these two problems:

Some writers have discussed the question from one point of view at one time and from another at another time. Other writers have confused the two points of view, but have allowed one of them to dominate their discussion. In still other cases a writer has treated the matter exclusively from one point of view. The first of these comments applies to Smith and J.S. Mill, the second to the Ricardians and the third to Jevons.

Within this framework, Buchanan's historical approach to rent theory is to assess the extent to which various writers tackle the problems with the solutions that are suggested by 'the equilibrium theory of value and distribution' to which he subscribes himself. This is a popular but misguided method of approach to the history of economic thought or indeed to the history of any discipline. As we observed in the opening chapter, the doctrines of the past should not be seen as an evolutionary path to those of the present. Buchanan's historical approach is to impose one theory upon others as if all were using the same concepts and posing the same problems.

The way in which he does this is instructive. Necessarily, it involves the reduction of the differences between theories on all matters relating to rent to the difference between allowing alternative land use or not. Correspondingly, where rent does enter into the price of a commodity, a writer must be considering the existence of competing land use and the allowance for an opportunity cost of alternative land use. Where rent does not enter into the price of a commodity, it must be the price of the only commodity being produced on the land as far as the particular author under consideration is concerned. The only other alternative is that a writer must be making a mistake or suffering from confusion. Thus 'Mill was an accomplished logician and it is unbelieveable that he, a life-long supporter of the Ricardian position, would publish in the same chapters in which he upheld that theory another theory which, *on the same hypotheses*, upheld the opposite. We have shown that the hypotheses were different and it appears clear that Mill recognized them to be so.' Here Buchanan presumes that apart from the universal validity of his own economic theory, there is a universal logic of which Mill is a master. Hence Mill must be in agreement with Buchanan. In fact, Mill is caught in a contradictory confusion brought about by his straddling the fence dividing classical political economy from marginalism, a process of the mixing of theories that is paralleled and perfected by Buchanan.

The basic problem for Buchanan, of the distinction between theory with alternative land use and without an alternative, is mirrored by the distinction between exchange and distribution, 'since the question of rent and price properly lies in two main fields, namely exchange and distribution.' It is not clear why production, however conceived, is excluded by Buchanan from being an element of rent and price theory. For him it should enter but merely as the technical conditions of production relating land as an input to one or more outputs, rather than as the social conditions governing access to land as a means of production.

Exchange theory, that is *relative* prices, corresponds to the existence of alternative land uses from which distribution theory is derived since rents (and wages and profits for that matter) are simply the prices of lands (and labour and capital). On the other hand, in the case of a single commodity, exchange theory necessarily evaporates leaving a residue consisting of distribution theory. Consequently, Buchanan should not have argued that the question of rent and price properly lies in the two main fields of exchange and distribution, but that it lies in the one or the other in exact correspondence to the existence of alternative land use or not.

This view is borne out by Buchanan's treatment of the historical elements in the distribution theories of rent. They are characterized by considerations of social classes, necessarily of landlords, and are thereby associated with Physiocracy. Thus, the single product theory of rent comprises: the

single product/rent is price determined/class relations of distribution/
Physiocracy theory of rent. All of these characteristics come together, or not
at all, since they are derivative of the single land use assumption. For
Buchanan 'there is much in common between the point of view with which
they (Ricardians) approached the subject and the point of view of the Physiocrats, which also dominated Smith's second treatment (single land use).
Their discussions were dominated by the point of view of distribution
between social classes.'

Thus, in summary, for Buchanan there are two complementary theories
of rent, and each theorist can draw on the one, the other or both without
inconsistency although possibly making for confusion. In the following
sections we shall show that Buchanan's approach leads to profound errors
of interpretation of various theories of rent. In the next section we are predominantly concerned with Smith's theory, and in the section following
that, the marginalist theory that preceded Buchanan but which has also
been reconstructed as the modern theory of consumer surplus.

Smith's Theory of Rent

The Physiocratic theory of rent is not predominantly concerned, despite
Buchanan, with the distribution of a single product between classes.
Rather, it sees the agricultural surplus, which is appropriated in the form of
rent, as the means of employing non-agricultural labour (such as, but not
exclusively manufacturers). Thus, the size of the agricultural surplus, when
set against the level of subsistence, does determine distributional relations,
but more important it determines the potential non-agricultural population that can be sustained.

Now, as Buchanan observes, Smith is commonly considered inconsistent
in his treatment of rent and price. He stated both that rent was and that it
was not an element determining the price of commodities. For Buchanan
this inconsistency is explained away by the dichotomy between the two rent
questions. When rent was price determined for Smith, he was theorizing
Ricardian single land usage, but when rent was price determining, he was
concerned with alternative land usage. It is with this latter interpretation
that we disagree. In our view, Smith's theory of rent as price determining,
with rent as one of the elements in his components theory of price, is in part
motivated by an imposition of Physiocratic notions onto capitalism. It is an
imposition because the Physiocratic theory does not depend upon the
coexistence of wages and profits with the rent component, since it is predominantly concerned with the production that can be sustained by the
agricultural surplus. As Meek (1962) has shown in his work it is, in general
for Physiocracy more a case of agriculture versus manufacture, with little
distinction being made between worker and capitalist and therefore
between wages and profits. But for Smith, wages and profits could enter

into price as independent component parts without agriculture being the sole source of surplus. Consequently, the Physiocratic theory of value and rent cannot be embraced without modification. Yet it does enter into Smith's theory of rent as a price determining component quite independently of the possibility of alternative land usage. However, it is certainly not true that Smith's rent theory relies exclusively upon these Physiocratic notions. He also employs Ricardian concepts of differential rent, but these are in addition to and at times inconsistent with the Physiocratic theory. It should be observed that our view has become diametrically opposed to Buchanan's. Where for him, Smith's rent as a component part is derived from alternative land usage, for us it arises from single land usage, that is for Buchanan the class (Physiocratic) theory of rent.

To justify our interpretation of Smith and our criticism of Buchanan we begin with Chapter XI of Book I of *The Wealth of Nations*, entitled 'Of the Rent of Land'. Here Smith certainly begins with the often quoted observation that rent is price determined: 'High or low wages and profit are the causes of high or low price; high or low rent is the effect of it' (p. 249). For Buchanan, this can be safely interpreted as the case of single land use and he passes over the next 'two "parts" which have little bearing upon our problem.' In fact, we shall find these parts are crucial, but first we should note that the causal relation between rent and price quoted above is not for Smith as simple as it seems. For it is discussed in the context of the suggestion that some commodities always pay a rent, and some do so only sometimes. Thus, whether there is rent at all or not depends upon the product and not upon the price. Once we have decided that a product always bears a rent then we can determine whether it is high or low according to the product's price. This view of Smith's would be consistent with Buchanan's if the irreducible rent of products that always bear one were determined by the opportunity cost of alternative land usage. This cannot be so. For the necessary rent is one that is paid for the use of land on which is grown the product that always affords a rent, whereas other commodities may not afford rent and therefore cannot set a standard of rent through competition for alternative land usage.

If Buchanan's interpretation of Smith cannot be correct, it remains to demonstrate the Physiocratic element of Smith's theory as we have understood it. This is relatively easy, if we do not ignore the parts that Buchanan correctly observes have 'little bearing upon our problem.' Part I of Chapter XI is entitled 'Of the Produce of Land which always affords Rent.' It is concerned with food, that is with subsistence, since 'land in its original rude state can afford the materials of clothing and lodging to a much greater number of people than it can feed' (p. 266). Whether the common food be corn, beef or potatoes, 'land in almost any situation, produces a greater quantity of food than what is sufficient to maintain all the labour necessary for bringing it to market, in the most liberal way in which that labour is ever maintained. The surplus, too, is always more than sufficient to replace the stock which employed that labour, together with its profits. *Something, therefore, always remains for a rent to the landlord*' (p. 250, emphasis added).

In Smith's theory, then, rent is first determined by absolute fertility in the production of labourer's food:

A rice field produces a much greater quantity of food than the most fertile corn field . . . Though its cultivation . . . requires more labour, a much greater surplus remains after maintaining all that labour. In those rice countries, therefore, where rice is the common and favourite vegetable food of the people, and where the cultivators are chiefly maintained with it, a greater share of this greater surplus should belong to the landlord than in corn countries (p. 263).

However, because rice is produced in bogs, its land has no alternative use, but the principles of rent determination have remained the same as for corn even though alternative land use cannot serve as the basis for calculating other rents:

A good rice field . . . is unfit for corn, or pasture, or vineyard, or, indeed, for any other vegetable produce that is very useful to men; and the lands which are fit for those purposes are not fit for rice. Even in the rice countries, therefore, the rent of rice lands cannot regulate the rent of the other cultivated land, which can never be turned to that produce (p. 264).

Buchanan cannot possibly be right in his interpretation of Smith's rent theory, since the Physiocratic element correctly understood is present whether there is alternative land use or not.

We conclude this section with some further comment on Smith's rent theory and contrast his theory with Ricardianism with which it was followed. In Part II of Chapter XI, Smith considers those products that may but do not necessarily afford rent. Essentially, he applies Ricardian principles of differential rent but he does not do so exclusively. This leads to some confusion in establishing which coal mine, for example, determines the price of output as opposed to the process by which that mine itself establishes the price. Competition, particularly when superior mines are brought into production, tends to eliminate the inferior mines so that for Smith the most fertile mine establishes price rather than the least fertile as demanded by the Ricardian principles. Compounding this confusion is Smith's reluctance to rely upon the Ricardian principles exclusively, since he is concerned with property rights on the land. Some mines (in Scotland) may 'afford some profit to the undertaker of the work, but no rent to the landlord. They can be wrought advantageously by nobody but the landlord . . . (who) will allow nobody else to work them without paying some rent, and nobody can afford to pay any' (p. 270). 'At a coal-mine for which the landlord can get no rent, but which he must either work himself or let it alone altogether, the price of coals must generally be nearly about this price' (p. 272). Yet, on the very same page, Smith asserts that 'the most fertile coal-mine, too, regulates the price of coals at all the other mines in its neighbourhood.'

Leaving aside this latter statement, whose source is a confusion identified above, the question is why Smith does not argue that the price of coal is exactly at the level determined by the no rent land, as Ricardo interprets him to do so and would have him do so:

After Adam Smith has declared that there are some mines which can only be worked by the owners . . . we should expect that he would admit that it was these particular mines which regulated the price of production from all mines (*Principles*, p. 331)

The answer is that Smith is concerned with property rights; the landlord will not let another onto the land without paying a rent so that if the landlord does not work the land, it is left unworked or a rent is paid pushing up the price by the amount of that rent. This last possibility is not openly admitted by Smith since he has already confusedly expected the most fertile mine to regulate the price. However, this regulated price includes a rent payment determined at the outside by the price of wood which is preferable to coal as a fuel and whose cultivation is substitutable for corn or pasture and whose rent is thereby determined according to the Physiocratic principle (p. 271). Thus, determination of price by the most fertile mine is consistent with rent on the least fertile, a rent that has to be paid to use the land.

The purpose of extending our interpretation of Smith to allow rent on all land, even in the absence of the Physiocratic element in the production of food, is to show that non-Ricardian rent arises even in the absence of that element. But another element takes its place, that of the capitalist independent of the constraint of landed property, for this is precisely what constitutes the landlord acting as his own proprietor. For another capitalist to take his place, a rent must be paid even if the land would otherwise lie idle. In this case, just as in the Physiocratic element of Smith's theory of rent, price must include rent as a determining component quite apart from Buchanan's considerations of alternative land usage.

We are now in a position to see the complexity of Smith's rent theory and, because of its diverse elements, the source of its confusions. Smith is seeking to understand rent in the context of a capitalist economy. In doing so, he draws directly upon an understanding of capitalism itself, for example in constructing price from wages, profits and rents. However, he also imposes upon capitalism an understanding drawn from other modes of production or from underdeveloped capitalism as in the Physiocratic theory of rent. Further he confronts a capitalism in which landlords work their own land with one in which they do not. The result is not simply confusion, but an important divergence from Ricardian rent theory. For, it is because Smith draws upon different modes of organizing production, that capital is confronted in his theory by landed property. Capitalists must pay a rent to use land and this is the source of Smith's rent as a determining component of price. His element of Physiocracy applied to capitalism insists that this absolute rent must exist, although the Ricardian element of this theory tends to deny it except when the landlord alone is able to work the land.

In complete contrast, Ricardo and the Ricardians expunge the Physiocratic element from their theory. For them, rent arises out of the (relative) natural conditions of fertility and situation, independently of landownership. The latter simply determines who will receive the rent. Buchanan's own rent theory, in both its versions, shares the Ricardian characteristic of being independent of landownership and this is true of neo-classical rent theory in so far as it exists. For this reason, it becomes impossible for Buchanan to interpret Smith's rent theory correctly. The absence of the effects of landed property in Buchanan means that its presence within Smith can only be erroneously seen as being derived from the availability of alternative land usage.

Following Ricardo then, rent theory, whether allowing alternative land usage or not, has been constructed in the absence of the effects of landownership. This makes impossible Buchanan's project of comprehending Smith's theory which does introduce such effects.

Marginalist Rent Theory

We have already seen that one crucial logical implication of the marginalist system is that the different sources of factor income are conceptually distinguishable only in so far as the conditions governing supply and demand are differentiated. This is why Hobson (1891) refers to 'the law of the three rents' and Clark (1891) sees 'distribution as determined by a law of rent.' For Walras (1954), rent is a 'part of the expenses of production at every moment of time exactly as every other outlay is . . .' and Jevons (1970) argues that 'so far as costs of production regulates the value of commodities, wages must enter into the calculation on exactly the same footing as rent.' In addition, the factor incomes are determined simultaneously, with their ultimate effect to be measured in terms of the individual utility generated. This involves what Fetter (1901) termed 'the passing of the old rent concept' which relied upon the Ricardian notion of a differential surplus measured exclusively in terms of the conditions of supply rather than the satisfaction of demand. The passage of the old concept has reached its perfection only in modern times, for reasons that will be discussed in this section. The modern theory of consumer surplus has formalized the conclusions implicit in the early marginalist theory by taking 'rent as a measure of welfare change'. It does so by abandoning the Marshallian concept of producers' surplus altogether since this is a more general instance of the

Ricardian differential in production. As we shall see in more detail later, the measurement of the economic surplus must be derived from individual utility gains calculated from a general equilibrium for which producer surplus cannot be defined.

Buchanan, however, interprets the early marginalists differently. He recognizes general equilibrium: that 'the essence of that theory is that *no expenses determine prices*, but that prices of production and rewards of productive agents are *mutually* determining.' But in utilizing his theory of alternative land use, Buchanan focuses exclusively upon the *supply* of alternative crops, a partial equilibrium. Thus land is treated equally to other factors of production only in terms of substitution in supply rather than in demand as a means of providing utility. This creates the illusion that a theory of rent has been constructed (just as marginal products of capital or labour would create the impression that profits or wages had been uniquely explained). Consequently, the marginalists, particularly Jevons, are interpreted as if they provide a theory of rent whereas we have argued in the previous chapter that the effect of marginalism is to eradicate the distinction that can be drawn between rent and other sources of factor income. Buchanan leaves the false impression that marginalism has a theory of rent which is produced by the consideration of alternative land usage. This is, however, no more a special theory of rent than the alternative uses of capital and labour constitute *separate* theories of profit and wages. Buchanan is caught in the marginalist dilemma. He accepts general equilibrium theory for which there is no special theory of rent and for which prices, including that of land, are all determined simultaneously. Yet he also wants a theory of rent and attempts to reach a compromise over what he recognizes to be an erroneous debate concerning whether rent is price determining or price determined. He does so by constructing a correspondence between these determinations and the availability or not of alternative land usage. Thereby a theory of rent appears to have been provided, but it is at the expense of general equilibrium and a retreat into partial equilibrium. For the two versions of rent theory either require a single good or for the price of alternative land use to be fixed.

In his article then, Buchanan did not seek simply to resolve a conflict between classical and neo-classical rent theory. By introducing his two problems and their solutions he sought to close a debate that had taken place within neo-classical economics itself. The early marginalists had generalized Ricardian rent notions to the economy as a whole thereby undermining the possibility of a theory specifically of rent. This is the logical conclusion to which general equilibrium is forced and it explains in part the almost total disappearance of rent as a current subject of economic theory. His contemporary economists, however, were dissatisfied with this result for two reasons. First, rent was recognized to be a uniquely defined factor income and secondly, it has a special relationship to land.

The problems with Buchanan's analysis are found to recur.

Marshall in particular clung to the notion of Ricardian rent and managed to do so by two devices. The first involved specifying the special conditions of land supply which various authors have usually characterized as indestructibility and fixed supply. By contrast, capital could be specified uniquely in terms of its productivity over time and dependence upon abstinence (waiting), and labour was defined in terms of its disutility and sacrifice of leisure. For Marshall (1893) utilizing the concept of producer surplus ('a convenient name for the genus of which the rent of land is the leading species' p. 76) the question of time was crucial for the distinction between rent and quasi-rent because land could not be expanded in supply whereas capital could, to eliminate quasi-rent. Unfortunately, this special property of land as a means to generate a special factor income depended upon Marshall's second device, the use of partial equilibrium analysis. Clearly, the measurement of the producer surplus depends upon the rest of the economy being exogenously fixed or the presupposition of a one good world. Otherwise rent as a factor income can only be derived from the set of equilibrium prices.

What we have seen is that Marshall failed to produce a theory of rent within general equilibrium theory. Neo-classical theory has compromised over this situation by abandoning general equilibrium whenever a theory of rent is required and otherwise adopting a theory of consumer surplus, even occasionally recognizing its schizophrenia. Thus Brown (1941) in response to Boulding (1941) (but see also (1945)) asks: 'Is the expression 'economic rent' now to do the duty for every sense in which we may say there is a 'surplus'? If so, what can the economist who believes the distinction between income from landownership and other income to be important do about the matter?'

This concern with rent as a factor income in the theory of distribution has recurred from time to time, most notably following Mishan's (1968) criticism of the notion of producers' surplus and when it has been rediscovered that there are historically two theories of rent. (See Mishan (1959), (1968) and (1969) and Wessel (1967) and (1969) and also the debate in the *Southern Economic Journal* in the early 1970s.) It became usual to refer back to Ricardo and Pareto as the sources of the two rent theories and Buchanan has been ignored. Essentially Mishan has rediscovered the early marginalist position in which final utility is the ultimate measure of economic activity and the laws of distribution are all equivalent to the one rent theory. His opponents in an ensuing debate have rediscovered the marginalists who reacted against this euthanasia for rent theory as a specific source of revenue tied to the land. At times the arguments may be more technically sophisticated but the conundrums remain the same and unresolved. As we have already observed, those theories that produce a distinct notion of rent are incompatible with general equilibrium theory either presuming a one good world or that the opportunity cost of alternative land use is already determined. Only if it recognizes a distinct role for landed property can economic theory construct a notion of rent that distinguishes it from other factor incomes. Otherwise, only by hopping from partial to general equilibrium, from a one to a many good world, can it create the illusion of having explained rent as a distinct source of income.

Further Reading

We recommend Buchanan's article 'The Historical Approach to Rent and Price Theory,' *Economica* (1929), for its gathering of the conflicting elements of neo-classical rent theory. As observed, these conflicts are only resolved by abandoning rent theory or by abandoning neo-classical economics. Otherwise the references in the text may be taken up according to the reader's interest.

8
On the Law of the Tendency of the Rate of Profit to Fall

Classical Political Economy and the Falling Rate of Profit

Each writer in the tradition of classical political economy took a position on the nature and causes of the laws governing the movement in the rate of profit. These are relatively easy to bring out on the basis of our earlier analyses of classical political economy. Adam Smith sees the accumulation of capital to be governed by the extent of the market and the growing division of labour. As the latter ultimately exhausts the former, the economy comes to rest with profitability reduced to a minimum. Smith's views can be interpreted in a number of ways. That profitability is limited by overall aggregate demand would reflect a focus upon the extent of the market. That the opportunities for extending the division of labour are exhausted would suggest a diminishing return to capital, although this is an argument that only applies to a single sector of the economy and is only erroneously extended to the economy as a whole. For the expansion of all sectors is the expansion of the market for each. There is some difficulty in justifying Smith's theory of the falling rate of profit except through the notion of absolute limits to either the extent of the market or to the division of labour or to both in their mutual interrelation.

What is absent from Smith's theory and is to be found in Ricardo's is a natural basis for postulating a falling rate of profit. As we have seen, Ricardo's theory of rent and its relation to accumulation depends upon diminishing returns in agriculture. Because corn forms a necessary component of the wage bundle, the value of corn increases with the accumulation of capital and with it the value of wages increases at the expense of profitability. Ultimately then the rate of profit is forced down to a minimum. Here Ricardo's theory is dependent upon declining productivity in agriculture.

Laws governing the rate of profit have gone out of fashion in modern economics. The sort of arguments employed by Smith involving the extent of the market have been incorporated into macro-economic theory by use of the concept of effective demand without any necessary reference to profitability. The role of the division of labour has been ignored. The passing of the quantitative importance of agriculture as a sector in the economy has appeared to render Ricardo's theory redundant. In any case, the existence of diminishing returns in agriculture can be questioned empirically given the high levels of productivity increases gained over the years, particularly on the intensive margin. However, Ricardo's result is reproduced in a neo-classical form from time to time. This theory, in a one-sector model, relates a falling rate of profit to a declining marginal productivity of capital as the capital-labour ratio increases. Capital as a whole now replaces Ricardo's agricultural sector as represented by corn. But the result is not robust without the assumption of a one-good world, as the Cambridge critique of capital theory has demonstrated.

This critique is itself the basis for an explanation of falling profitability that is reminiscent of Ricardo's theory but in a different way. It explains falling profitability by rising wages, but these are in turn caused by class distributional struggle rather than 'natural' rises in the value of corn. In other words, the natural basis in Ricardo for rising wages, the meeting of subsistence requirements with a declining productivity of agriculture, is replaced by a social basis, the demands of workers for increasing wages. It is this which attaches a flavour of Marxist political economy to a Ricardian root. Marx himself both rejects the view that there is declining productivity in agriculture and that rising wages are a systematic cause of falling profitability. This makes it impossible for those following Marx to prove in a mathematical sense that the rate of profit must fall. It has led to a debate over the status of the law of the tendency of the rate of profit to fall, what was for Marx the most important law of political economy. The remainder of this chapter will be devoted to one particular part of the debate over the law. In doing this, it should be borne in mind that the law derives its significance for Marxism from its relation to an explanation of the causes of crises. This is quite easily forgotten as the focus moves from crisis as such to a preoccupation with movements in the rate of profit. It is often presumed that a fall in profitability is the necessary and theoretical result, since a crisis would be the necessary consequence. This, however, cannot be taken for granted, as we shall see.

Okishian Theory

In the previous section, it was shown that classical political economy relies for a theory of the falling rate of profit upon declining productivity or upon limited markets. In the absence of either of these two causes, some have argued that the only source of a falling rate of profit is increasing wages. This is a view that parallels Ricardo's for whom increasing wages in value terms expressed the declining productivity of corn. In more modern versions, the theory would locate the source of increasing wages in a decline in the reservoirs of labour supply as accumulation proceeds or in an increasing militancy in wage bargaining from the working class.

Within this framework of analysis of movements in the rate of profit, a slightly different approach has been taken by economists whom we shall label Okishians because they follow the theory put forward by Okishio (1961). Rather than analysing the effect of increasing wages on profitability, they examine the effect of changing technology when wages remain the same. Their purpose in doing so is to question what they take to be Marx's theory of the law of the tendency of the rate of profit to fall (LTRPF). For them, Marx's theory depends upon individual capitalists choosing less costly methods of production as they accumulate, in contrast say to Ricardo for whom the extensive margin in agriculture guarantees increasing costs.

The Okishians raise the question of whether, when capitalists are able to and do adopt less costly and hence more profitable techniques individually, they are nevertheless faced with a fall in the rate of profit as a whole. This may appear to be impossible on a trivial level. If each individual capitalist adopts more profitable methods, profitability as a whole must increase. But things are not quite that simple. When all the capitalists in one or more sectors have adopted new techniques, the whole structure of prices is changed throughout the economy and the effect on the rate of profit is not immediate. For example, at existing wages and prices, a capitalist in the steel industry makes an extra profit by introducing a new technique. When all other capitalists in the steel sector adopt this technique, profitability is restored to normal by a reduction in the price of steel. This in turn affects the profitability and prices of all commodity producers using steel until it reaches those producers using those commodities using steel. Ultimately new levels of prices and profits are established.

What will have happened to the level of profitability? The Okishians show that the intuition to be drawn from the experience of the first innovating capitalist is appropriate for the fate of capital as a whole. When all is said and done, the effect of a technical change which lowers the cost of one or more commodities must raise the rate of profit if the level of wages is held constant. From this, further conclusions can be drawn: that the rate of profit can only fall if the level of wages rises so that increasing wages must be the cause of falling profitability, provided there has not been any decline in techniques available.

The Okishians depend upon simple mathematical results derived from the relationships between uniform levels of wages, prices and profits given underlying technical relations between inputs and outputs. As an economic method this deserves a closer interrogation. If the mathematics is beyond dispute, the method of the Okishians (and more generally of the Sraffians of whom they form a part) can be characterized as vulgar in that it draws no distinction between the status of the concepts employed. There is no reality and appearance distinguished. The various categories of wages, prices and profits are presumed to exist along with the technical relations by which they are calculated. This implies that the theory contains empirical material drawn from capitalist society but only in a way which accords it an equal conceptual status to non-capitalist, general categories such as labour and technology. Nevertheless, there is a causative structure within the theory, but this is itself open to criticism. Since wages, prices and profits are calculated (that is determined mathematically) on the basis of exogenously determined technical relations, changes in technology give rise to changes in wages, prices and profits. Consequently, changes in technology cause changes in other economic variables. Causation coincides with the calculation from exogenously given factors.

What is unsatisfactory with this method is that the causative elements are outside the theory itself. By the very way in which they cause change within the theory, they are excluded from being analysed by the theory. Consequently, technical changes, accumulation (to increase the demand for labour and hence wages) and class struggle to increase wages are introduced from outside the theory even though they are the most important causative elements within it. The same must be said of the empirical element incorporated. The exchange categories of capitalism such as prices, wages and profits, only enter the theory in order that they may be calculated; otherwise they have no causative significance.

This is not quite correct because, as we have seen in the first chapter, theories built on models such as these have both an external and an internal causative content. The latter is derived from the conceptual understanding drawn from the relations between the endogenous variables in their dependence upon the exogenous variables. The source of this causative content in general is the extent to which variables are treated as having a social existence which is independent of and therefore determines their relation to their aggregated and complex individualized existence. We have given examples of this in chapter 1, and the Okishian theory provides us with another.

The specific form that this takes for the Okishians is almost brought out into the open by Roemer (1979) when he demands that Marxist macro-economics should be consistent with its micro-economic foundations. What he means by this is that the macro-economic aggregates of Marxist theory should be built up from the micro-economic behaviour of individuals. This is exactly the reversal of Marx's method which is to proceed from the simplest aggregate categories, such as capital and labour, and to reproduce these at a more complex and concrete level, the 'micro-economics'. It is also a departure from Marx's method in not distinguishing between the conceptual status of the macro- and micro-economic levels of analysis, in the simplest terms, leaving no difference between reality and appearance. For Marx, this is the method of 'vulgar' economics and it is one whose micro-foundations and hence its macro-economics, are rooted in the analysis of exchange relations. Taken to its logical conclusion, it concerns itself with and differentiates every single individual act of exchange within the economy. Clearly Roemer and the other Okishians do not reproduce a model of such generality and open superficiality. Certain uniformities are taken to exist between different acts of exchange. These are that exchanges take place at uniform levels of prices, wages and profits. These exchanges are taken to be social categories but their relationship to their micro-foundations is not questioned, even though each act of exchange is potentially at a different price, wage or profit level.

Of course, these assumptions are justified by an appeal to the effects of perfect competition. But this competition takes place at the level of individual acts of exchange where the tendency for divergence must be as great or at least exist as much as the tendency for uniformity. The assumption of uniformity then constrains these potential differences to evaporate and leaves behind a causative content. For it leads to the conclusion that exchange of labour takes place between capital as a whole and labour as a whole and that the resulting profits and prices are a consequence of a confrontation between the two classes over this exchange. In fact, the micro-foundations should suggest otherwise: that exchange does not take place between the classes and that it is potentially at different levels of wages. Indeed, this is a line of pursuit for the Sraffian theory of segmented labour markets which, taken to its logical conclusion, would have every labourer in his or her own labour market. Paradoxically, it is only the introduction of competition between individuals to make prices etc. uniform, which makes it appear as if exchanges take place between classes. In this sense, the theory is inconsistent for taking the exchange of labour as both taking place between individuals and between classes. This does indeed occur in the real world, since both classes and individuals exist. The individual acts of exchange over the level of wages in this context reproduce at a more complex level the act of exchange between capital and labour over the value of labour-power. This is the class-based macro-foundation of the micro-economy for Marxism, although it appears to the Okishians that the reverse method should be employed.

That the Okishian derivation of a causative relation between wages and profits is conceptually unsatisfactory can be seen in another way. Logically, there is no reason why the wage-profit relation should be seen as determinant. The system could be closed in many other ways than fixing a level of wages through class struggle. The particular owners of the commodity labour are afforded a privilege which could as well belong to the owners of any other commodity. Ricardo's theory of accumulation could be interpreted in this way, since it is a rising price of corn that determines everything else. The particular causative role assigned to the wage-profit relation in Okishian theory then assigns price a lower status than wages (and profits) even though wages as the price of labour and profits as the price of capital are themselves prices within the theory.

It might be argued that these criticisms are relatively insignificant since it is in some sence more 'realistic' to assume that there are uniform prices etc., than there are not. This objection, however, misses the point. Ultimately, 'realism' of this type does involve the movement to more and more complex concepts but only at the expense and elimination of the simpler ones. It is analogous to denying the existence of class relations because there are fractions of classes and leads to analysis based on individuals. It allows class relations within the theory only by a sleight of hand, by treating individuals as though they were all the same so that there can be representative workers and capitalists to make the exchange over wages between capital and labour. These are classes treated as though they were individuals, struggling over the division of surplus product because of their symmetrical relationship in the monopsony ownership of capital and labour.

It is well-recognized that the Okishians' analysis is an exercise in comparative statics. After an exogenous change in a parameter, namely technology, the economy settles down to a new equilibrium which can be compared with the former one. It is found that if the wage level has not risen, the rate of profit cannot fall. This static comparison of equilibria has important implications for the quality of the theory. Even if we accept the existence of equilibrium, it most clearly diverts attention away from the dynamic passage from one equilibrium to the next. Here, the question of stability is ignored and can only be treated by introducing more assumptions about how the economy (or individuals) would behave out of equilibrium. This is difficult for this type of analysis. Implicitly, assumptions about individual behaviour have already been made, although this is concealed by the uniformity of their behaviour. Out of equilibrium, individuals no longer behave uniformly, so that different assumptions must be made. This is a problem because disparate patterns of behaviour displace the uniformities previously assumed and cannot be seen as a concretization of more fundamental underlying relations. More specifically, this concerns the concept of competition employed and will be taken up later.

Once we recognize in the Okishian theory that there is a dynamic problem of movement between equilibria which differ because of an exogenously introduced change in technology, then rather different questions might be posed. If the economy did not move towards the new equilibrium, or if the processes that produce technical change are themselves a function of being out of equilibrium, then how does the economy change? In either case, the results of comparative statics are worthless, since the equilibrium is never attained. In the case of technology changing outside equilibrium, it is not simply a failure to move to the new equilibrium, it is a movement towards or away from an equilibrium which is itself on the move. It might even be suggested that equilibrium does not exist, hardly an outrageous suggestion for those pursuing the Marxist tradition. Then what status remains for a theory that depends upon equilibrium concepts? It might be retorted that Marx's own analysis contains a core of equilibrium analysis, most notably in the economic reproduction of Volume II and the transformation of values into prices of production in Volume III. These are not, however, equilibrium analyses even though they can be so interpreted. These analyses concern not equilibrium quantities and prices, respectively, but the reproduction of simpler value concepts at a more complex level for which equilibrium is quite unnecessary.

The foregoing remarks on equilibrium are not novel and so have not gone completely unnoticed by the Okishians themselves. Parijs (1980) observes quite correctly that there is no immediate relation between a falling rate of profit and an economic crisis, no matter what causes the fall. Accumulation can proceed, no matter what is happening to the rate of profit, at the rate at which profits are invested. Marx observes that a fall in the rate of profit can produce a slackening of accumulation without the necessary intervention of crisis. There seems to be some agreement on this point even if the literature on the falling rate of profit has from many different standpoints taken its fall, to bring crises automatically. Yet, the way in which Parijs makes this simple point is symptomatic of the Okishian method, '. . . . it is impossible for a fall in the equilibrium rate of profit (due to a rise in the organic composition) to generate crises.' Most of this sentence is superfluous and what would remain is the simplest tautology. Can a change in *equilibrium* generate crises? 'It is impossible for . . . equilibrium . . . to generate crises.' p. 9.

The use of an equilibrium analysis has other drawbacks, not least of which is that the exclusion of dynamics is the exclusion of time. In a formal sense, time and its passage can be present within the theory. But the future and the present are connected together in exactly the same way as the present is connected to the past. As Sraffians have shown, the Okishians' analysis is based on dated labour-time discounted to its present value by the rate of interest. The rate of interest is itself taken to be identical to the rate of profit and this reflects the absence of money and credit within the theory. The important conclusion to emerge is that the present determines the future no more than the future determines the present (which it does not do at all). The future for the Okishians is the reproduction of the present just as the present is the reproduction of the past and the mechanism linking them through the passage of time is the rate of profit (interest). The rate of profit can only perform this function in equilibrium so that it is known in advance. Out of equilibrium, the rate of profit cannot serve this function of collapsing the future into the present since it has to be determined by how the present becomes the future. There is a separation in time and place between acts of production and acts of exchange so that all prices, as well as the rate of profit, are not determined simultaneously as in the Okishian theory. As the future does not reproduce the present, the connection between the two can only be established theoretically by a concept which is itself dynamic and subject to change. Otherwise there can be no analysis of how the present becomes the future, only at best how the future has already become the present.

While this may appear to be playing with words, it is otherwise. We have seen, for Smith in chapter 5 and for Sraffa and Ricardo in chapter 3, how important is the way in which time is incorporated into an economic theory. For an equilibrium analysis, it is necessarily one in which the relation between the present and the past is identical to the one between the future and the present. Consequently, the associated economic concepts will hardly be able to capture the essence of explaining an economic crisis.

Marx's Theory of the LTRPF

It is the absence of a (satisfactory) dynamics that limits the Okishian theory, not only in its own products, but in its interpretation of other theories. For the latter, any dynamic concept is necessarily misunderstood as a static equilibrium category. This is most relevantly demonstrated by the notion of the composition of capital, a concept which is crucial to Marx's theory. Marx defines the composition in three ways. The technical composition of capital (TCC), measures the mass of raw materials and depreciating fixed capital that are worked up per unit of living labour. The major part of Volume I of *Capital* is devoted to showing how the production of surplus value through the capitalistic seizure of the labour process leads to a rising TCC. The tendency for the TCC to rise then is not some logical possibility but is the form that productivity increase takes for capitalism, as machinery displaces living labour and increases the rate of the labourer's transformation of raw materials into final products in a given time.

The TCC can be calculated in value terms, not simply as a theoretical construct, but because value exists for capitalist production (i.e., products take the form of commodities so that exchange brings many different concrete labours into equivalence with each other). But the TCC in value terms in a dynamic context raises a theoretical problem. The very changes in the TCC that are to be measured by values are themselves associated with changes in those values as productivity is increased by the rising TCC. For this reason, Marx distinguishes the organic from the value composition of capital (OCC and VCC). The OCC is the direct reflection of the rising TCC leaving aside the value changes that it brings about. The VCC measures the TCC taking account both of the technical (or organic) as well as the value changes that the rising TCC produces.

For an equilibrium analysis, the distinction between the OCC and the VCC is pointless. As technical changes are immediately translated into value (or more exactly price and profit) changes, the two compositions are identical as they must be in a static formulation. Both are measured by C/V, the ratio of constant to variable capital, and what is actually the VCC is usually called the OCC since Marx expounded the law of the tendency of the rate of profit to fall (LTRPF) in terms of the OCC. The OCC as understood by Marx, is ghosted away in content and retained in name whilst the VCC suffers the reverse fate. This is precisely because of the translation of productivity change automatically and immediately into value change. Where the Okishians do refer to a distinction between the OCC and the VCC, it is not to introduce dynamics but to alter definitions for mathematical convenience. There is no way in which the dynamic content of the concepts utilized by Marx can be included within their theory.

Introducing the composition of capital here does not serve simply to expose the limitations of the Okishian equilibrium approach. It allows us to present briefly the nature of Marx's theory of the LTRPF, a theory that is necessarily open to misinterpretation by the Okishian use of an equilibrium analysis imposed upon a theory of accumulation. Marx's own presentation of the subject occupies three short chapters in Volume III of *Capital*. *The Law as Such* simply relates a tendency for the rate of profit to fall with a rising *OCC*. This is a law of capitalist *production* in the sense that it reflects the nature of the development of the production process as a relation between capital and labour as a result of the exchange of labour power between the two classes. This law could well have been presented at the end of Volume I, once the analysis of this relation between capital and labour had been developed. The same is not true of the *Counteracting Influences*. These depend upon the formation of values in exchange and so upon the relations between many capitals in competition. Volume II of *Capital* provides the basis for this by analysing economic reproduction of sectors and revenues through exchange, and Volume III begins by examining the formation of prices of production through a distribution of surplus value by an average rate of profit according to capital advanced. These are not simply quantitative relations but reveal the structures and processes by which the capital-labour relation is reproduced in a more complex form by the relations between many capitals.

The counteracting influences themselves are systematic products of the capitalist economy. Two, in particular, should command our attention. The rising TCC brings not only a rising OCC but also a reduction in values in the formation of the VCC. The values of constant and variable capital are both reduced and this tends to raise the rate of profit as a result of the production of relative surplus value. However, although the changing OCC and VCC are both associated with the rising TCC they are not both caused in the same way. As we have seen, the OCC concerns relations between capital and labour in production where value and surplus value are created. The VCC is only formed when these relations of production are expressed in exchange through the competition between capitals. There is not necessarily the automatic harmony between the two processes that is suggested by the Okishians.

This is the theme taken up by Marx in his third chapter on the *Exposition of the Internal Contradictions of the Law*. Here his focus is not upon the algebraic sum of the LTRPF and the counteracting influences to discover whether the rate of profit falls or not. Rather his question is whether the tendency and the counteracting influences can coexist as accumulation proceeds. His answer is that there are contradictions *between* the two and these must give rise to crises from time to time. In pursuing this theme, Marx is relatively unconcerned about the movements in the actual rate of profit except in so far as it stands as a terminological proxy for his primary question of whether accumulation can be sustained without a crisis.

As a result Marx's analysis has certain characteristics that are at odds with the Okishian interpretation of it. Marx's law does not concern immediate empirical movements and predictions of the rate of profit. Both it and the counteracting influences involve relatively simple concepts (the first more so than the second) and their interaction to produce a rate of profit involves a more complex analysis that examines the results of competition between capitals. Despite the abstract status of the theory, it is not without a predictive content, not least of which is the necessity of crises as the complex result of the coexistence of the tendency and counteracting influences.

Nor is Marx's theory concerned with secular or long run tendencies although his theory also has implications for these. Rather the LTRPF is linked to the capitalist cycle of production and so cannot be interpreted to be predicting a fall in the rate of profit over a hundred years or a rise in the OCC (or rather the VCC) over the same period. In looking at the cycle, Marx tends to examine the mass of surplus value and whether it can be accumulated, this expansion itself being based on a centralization of capital that forms a division between existing and newly formed or additions to capitals. The cycle is seen as a restructuring of capital, not as a quantitative equilibrium expansion, and is accomplished through exchange relations just as the OCC becomes transformed into the VCC through exchange. In more general terms, the rising OCC can be seen as the development of the forces of production which come into contradiction with the relations of production associated with the VCC, for the reproduction and transformation of value relations through accumulation is nothing short of the reorganization of the class relations between capital and labour through the circulation of capital.

In Marx's theory then, as capital is accumulated there is an expansion of surplus value production at the same time as values are being reduced. In the earlier chapter on Smith's value theory, we saw that Smith analyses this dynamic by the components theory of price which itself has problems associated with it, since the bypassing of constant capital allowed its value to change as if it had been produced under a future more developed division of labour. For Marx, it is the reduction in values as accumulation proceeds that tends to undermine the preservation of existing values and their embodiment in capital. This is why the LTRPF and the counteracting influences cannot coexist side by side in repose even during a phase of expansion: capitals are being devalued even as they are being preserved and expanded. The value that they represent decreases as living labour suffers relative expulsion from the production process. In a recession following a crisis, the decrease in the value of capitals is only achieved by the destruction of those capitals in the form of their lying idle. The restructuring of capital on the basis of a continued accumulation has proved incompatible with the means of reorganization through exchange.

The preceeding characterization of crises and their relation to the LTRPF is relatively mechanical. For it to be otherwise, the relation between the law and the counteracting influences must be produced at a more complex level. Here we indicate briefly how this can be done and the contribution that Marx makes. The law poses the need to examine the reorganization of production in its interaction with exchange. At the very simplest level this involves the question of value formation as value itself is changing. Just as different concrete labours are brought into equivalence through the exchange of commodities, so the value created by current living labour is brought into equivalence with what is now the productive labour of the past. As we have seen earlier in criticizing the equilibrium-based content of Okishian theory, dynamics requires the future to be connected to the present which produces it. The very problem of relating newly formed independent values to their dependence upon the preservation of old values might appear to question the validity of the concept of value itself. But there are two tendencies at work. One is to create new values which diverge from the old, the other is to establish the new values as socially necessary labour time for all producers. Moreover, the problem of what value is during the revolutions in values is itself solved within the capitalist economy by the form that values take in exchange, in their equivalence. Their value is represented by a quantity of money, and as Marx shows at the beginning of Volume I, money is the social form in which labour is represented. Consequently, the analysis of the LTRPF requires a theory of the value represented by money.

Money itself, however, has other properties. It is the form taken both in the advance of capitals and in the realization of commodities. The activities of interest-bearing capital and merchant capital to promote the centralization of capital and the realization of surplus value are themselves means of reorganizing production through exchange. Marx develops theories of both of these to show how they promote capital accumulation but in a way that is contradictory and subject to critically violent movements. These are intensified by the relative independence of exchange-based capitals which are open to speculation and the creation of illusory profits. The most significant divergence, however, between value preservation and value reduction occurs potentially for fixed capital since its turnover time exceeds the time even for which values are being reduced over a production period.

There is then further logical analysis possible for understanding the LTRPF as the law is reproduced more concretely by examining the capitalist mechanisms of exchange and competition. However, further concretization also requires the incorporation of more historical elements. At a particular time, the reorganization of capital tends to become concentrated in particular economic mechanisms and competition to be focused in particular forms, whether it be access to markets, finance or labour-power. This is true for particular epochs over which there may be a number of cycles as well for the characteristics of a particular cycle within an epoch. It is here that further historical insights must be incorporated into the more abstract tendencies.

Consequently, the incorporation of a dynamics and of time into the theory cannot be satisfactorily done by some simple modification of the Okishian concepts to produce·what neo-classical economics would term a disequilibrium theory. Rather, like other concepts examined in a different context, the abstractions involved must contain an empirical content of which historically evolved conditions are a part.

In this section, we have travelled a long way from the limitations of equilibrium analysis to the alternative theoretical methods and problems posed by examination of capital accumulation as a dynamic process. We began with a theory with exogenously determined wages and technology; without money; an automatic harmony between production, distribution and exchange; a rate of profit/interest connecting the present to an indistinguishable past and future. We have arrived with a relationship between money, value and capital at a simple level but whose complex reproduction opens up a theoretical challenge for further logical and historical analysis.

The Okishian Law of the Tendency of the Rate of Profit to Rise . . .

Sraffian criticisms of the LTRPF in the Okishian tradition take a number of forms. For example, that the TCC need not rise if capitalists choose 'capital-saving' technology. Here technology is assumed to be neutral in the sense of being able to change in any direction, hardly surprising if its changes are taken to be exogenous. Or that the OCC need not rise because of a greater cheapening of constant relative to variable capital. Here the OCC is confused with the VCC and the law as such with the counteracting influences. Or that the rate of exploitation rises and so the counteracting influences can outweigh the law. This treats the LTRPF as an empirical prediction rather than as an exposition of contradictory tendencies. Finally, the propositions of the law are examined against more or less long run empirical data and can be found to be wanting. This reveals again a misunderstanding of the status of the concepts employed and connects them with the most inappropriate empirical material.

These objections to the LTRPF are clumsy since they involve an attempt to reconcile a set of concepts drawn from one theory with those drawn from another. The Okishians eliminate this clumsiness (except when they claim to be reproducing Marx) by presenting their own theory of the rate of profit without the traditional fetters imposed by the heritage of Marx's own contribution. Then the rate of profit can be calculated on the basis of given wages and technology. Now suppose a new technique comes along that is more profitable than existing techniques. A capitalist adopts it and receives a higher rate of profit, at least temporarily. For reasons which will become clear later, we shall term this the law of the tendency of the rate of profit to rise (LTRPR). It is a very simple law, easily understood by any capitalist: reduced costs lead to increased profits. As long as there is technical progress, in the sense of the continuous availability of new techniques and no loss of old ones, the law appears to be a logical necessity.

It is, however, a law for individual capitalists. What is its significance for the economy as a whole? Here the Okishians are in their element. Once the new technique has become generalized to other capitals within the sector, then the new equilibrium will constitute a different pattern of prices and a different rate of profit. Whilst the new technique is only introduced by an individual capitalist on the basis of a profit increase in terms of the old prices, it nevertheless leads to an increase in profits for all capitalists when the economy settles down to the new equilibrium. The LTRPR does not appear to be merely a law nor a tendency but a cast-iron necessity. Let us, however, remind ourselves of the result. If technology improves between states of equilibrium with fixed levels of wages, then the rate of profit increases. But we have looked at LTRPR without looking at its counteracting influences separately.

. . . And the Counteracting Influences

The LTRPR is a law for individual capitalists. If any one of them introduces a new technique the individual rate of profit increases above the average. We shall consider the counteracting influences to be the effect that social capital has on individual capitalists in response to this. As capital flows into the sector with the new technique or capitalists there follow suit in introducing it, the price concerned is reduced and in the new equilibrium the innovator's profits once again become equalized to the (new) norm. What is complicated in all this is that the price reduction feeds itself back through the whole productive system reducing the costs of inputs and wages as a whole, increasing the rate of profit. As far as the individual innovating capitalist is concerned there is a burning question. Is the temporary surplus profit eroded or not? The answer is no and yes for the LTRPR and the counteracting influences, respectively. The LTRPR states immediately that profit is higher, but it can be shown that the higher rate of profit is eroded in the movement to the new equilibrium even if that new equilibrium has a higher general rate of profit than the old, as the Okishians prove in comparative statics. There are then counteracting influences to the LTRPR. These are due to the effects that social capital has on individual capitals by making uniform an initial advantage in technique.

In general, the Okishians have made very little attempt to study the LTRPR and the counteracting influences in isolation from each other. This follows from their preoccupation with comparative statics equilibrium analysis. The LTRPR is the dynamic involved in the introduction of new techniques by some capitalists and not by others. The counteracting influences also constitute a dynamic element, the catching up by the other capitalists whilst the innovators rest on their laurels, or more exactly their diminishing surplus profits. Then, the net result is that the LTRPR and the counteracting influences cancel out each other's dynamic to produce a new *equilibrium* in which the rate of profit is higher. This is most clear if we examine what is happening to individual profitability. From a situation in which it is uniform, the LTRPR produces a divergence between individual rates of profit. From this position, the counteracting influences restore uniform profitability. In each case, a dynamics is incorporated into the analysis because individual capitalists are affected differently. Yet the overall result is to reproduce equilibrium. It is one in which the LTRPR outweighs the counteracting influences. If individual capitalists represent the stars in the constellation of the economy, the LTRPR is associated with an opposite but diminished reaction from the counteracting influences in determining movements in profitability.

We are now in a position to compare the LTRPF with LTRPR. We can begin by simply pointing out their differences. We will see that each is the exact opposite of the other. The LTRPF is based on capital as a whole as a result of the developing relations between capital and labour as a whole in competition over the production of surplus value. The LTRPR is based upon individual capitals in competition introducing new techniques. The counteracting influences to the LTRPF concern the effects of the laws of production on many capitals in competition. The counteracting influences to the LTRPR concern the effect of many capitals in competition upon individual capitals. The LTRPF takes the dynamics of capitalist production and reproduces it at the more complex level of many capitals through its interaction with the counteracting influences. The LTRPR takes the dynamics of individual capitals and lays it side by side with the counteracting influences of the dynamics of many capitals and brings the economy to a state of rest. The LTRPF is an abstract law whose interaction with the counteracting influences can only be examined by further logical and historical analysis at a more complex level. The LTRPR is an immediate law whose interaction with the counteracting influences can only be examined by rejecting the simpler (but nevertheless vulgar) abstract categories, such as uniform wages, profits and prices, and introducing divergencies between these to reflect competition.

Finally consider the status of each as a law. The LTRPR reveals nothing that is hidden. The exact opposite is true of the LTRPF, and nothing could exemplify this more than its struggle against the LTRPR. What is true for social capital appears to be the opposite to the individual capitalist. The LTRPF appears as a profit increase to the individual capitalist introducing a productivity increase. The counteracting influences appear as a downward pressure on profits as prices decrease. Throughout his presentation of the law, Marx refers to the way in which it appears reversed in the process of competition, in the eyes of an individual capitalist. Although his remarks are short and directed more against classical political economy than the Okishians, Marx anticipates their theory but only as the form of appearance of his own, so that the LTRPR is the vulgar form of the LTRPF.

Okishian Dynamics

We have observed earlier that the Okishians tend to neglect the dynamics of the transition between one equilibrium and another. There are good reasons for this. Crucial to the Okishian determination of prices is the role played by individual capitals in competition. This appears otherwise because competition is made to make wage and profit rates uniform, only technology and the wage rate is needed. Conceptually, however, competition has already been introduced to determine prices. This stands in strong contrast to Marx's (and Ricardo's) value theory where prices of production are determined by value relations alone. Competition between individual capitalists then concerns the deviation of individual values from sectoral values and sectoral market prices from prices of production once the average rate of profit is formed.

For the Okishians the difficulty of dynamics is that competition has already been introduced to determine equilibrium prices, so that competition cannot be used to analyse the consequences of the deviation of prices from equilibrium prices without violating the initial competitive assumptions. At best there can be a hierarchy of assumptions about competition. The norm is perfect competition, the abnormal any deviation from this and there are many possibilities. It is logically arbitrary, although the assumptions are dictated by the model and notions of 'realism'. This is a situation comparable to the problems with Smith's notion of the divergence of market from natural price, noted in chapter 5.

These remarks are relevant to a dispute that has taken place recently in the *Cambridge Journal of Economics*. Whilst commenting upon Dobb's contribution to crisis theory, Anwar Shaikh makes a critique of Okishian theory. He wished to show that even if wages were to remain constant, a falling rate of profit could result from the availability and introduction of new techniques. Because of the Okishian result, this could only be done by adopting a theory in which capitalists do not choose to maximize the rate of profit. This is the option chosen by Shaikh (1978) and reconfirmed in the reply to his critics (1980).

He does this by drawing the distinction between unit cost price and discounted cost price in the presence of fixed capital. Unit cost is simply the average cost of production taking account of the spreading of fixed capital costs over the total output produced. This diverges from the discounted cost because the fixed capital costs must be evaluated for the time for which they are advanced. Now consider the choice of technique between two alternative production processes. The traditional approach has been to argue that the one chosen will have the higher rate of profit and this is an identical criterion to choosing on the basis of the lower discounted cost price. Shaikh argues against this criterion as follows. In anticipation of a lowering rate of profit as prices fall in the battle of competition to sell commodities, the criterion of least unit cost is more appropriate. For, if prices and the rate of profit do fall, then profitability will be higher for the more fixed capital intensive methods of production despite lower current profitability. This is because the discounting of the heavier fixed capital expenditures takes place at a lower discount rate. Indeed, it is possible that at the lower prices and profitability, the more labour-intensive technique will even make a loss. Consequently capitalists will choose techniques in order to give the lowest unit cost rather than discounted cost. By doing so, the rate of profit itself may fall because its increase is no longer the criterion of choice of technique.

What are we to make of Shaikh's argument? Despite the fact that it is critical of the Okishian theory, it is important to emphasize that it rests within its tradition and does not depart from it. What Shaikh has observed is the counteracting influences to the LTRPR. These observations he passes onto the individual capitalists within his theory. They in turn take fright and do not behave according to the principles of the LTRPR. Rather they adopt a policy of unit cost minimization rather than of profit maximization. But, although this restores a falling profitability and is consistent with the increasing use of machinery (fixed capital), it represents neither Marx's method nor LTRPF.

This is because Shaikh, like the Okishians, proceeds to determine the economy from the behaviour of individual capitalists. The strength of his analysis is to reject comparative statics and to ask what do capitalists do when faced with competition. He proposes an answer that diverges from the traditional one and as such is a contribution to the managerial theory of the firm. In doing so, he creates more problems than he solves. The first concerns price determination itself, including thereby the rate of profit. If capitalists govern their own behaviour by unit costs rather than by profitability, then it is not clear why profits would be distributed according to capital advanced to form prices of production. Capital would flow to equalize profit margins over unit costs (see Steedman (1980)). Nor is it clear why falling profitability should lead to a crisis, since this is what capitalists are anticipating and reorder their criterion of choice accordingly. In short, Shaikh's analysis rather leaves value and price determination up in the air, a problem that he acknowledges in response to a comment of Eatwell's and which is also noticed by Steedman. Shaikh's suggestion is that this still needs to be worked out at a greater level of complexity which differentiates capitalists in their use of techniques etc. But this is pre-empted by his already being at that level of analysis for which capitals are in competition.

It is also unclear why capitalists should be exclusively obsessed with the counteracting influences to the LTRPR. Price decreases for their own product suggest comparable changes in other markets reducing input costs (the force of Bleaney's (1980) comment) and lowering wage costs for real wages to remain the same (Nakatani (1980)). The assumption of constant uniform real wages in the Okishian theory is then seen to depend not only upon an exchange between capital and labour but also upon a compensating change in money wages whenever the prices of consumption goods change. This is itself problematical in the absence of a theory of money.

Given all these considerations, it is not clear why the counteracting influences should dominate the LTRPR in the minds of the capitalists. Nor is it clear that there is liable to be a major conflict between criteria of minimization of unit costs and profit maximization. It is most likely that the introduction of machinery will satisfy both. (Otherwise long abandoned labour intensive techniques are more profitable than current ones but too risky!)

There is an interesting parallel between Shaikh's arguments and those of Smith. Both tend to be blinkered by the effects of other sectors as they determine profitability by the ability to sell within the sector. But price changes come from other sectors also. The same is true for an expanding demand from other sectors so that the extent of the market need obstruct neither the division of labour nor the pursuit of profitability. This parallel with Smith is one that is carried over into the role played by the rate of interest. In his considerations on the rate of profit Smith finds it extremely uneven between capitalists and highly volatile over time. Consequently, he takes the rate of interest as a proxy for it. Shaikh does much the same thing and introduces the rate of interest as the basis for discounting fixed capital costs (see also Armstrong and Glyn (1980) who maximize individual profitability on this basis). Yet the rate of interest only appears to be the simplest of categories because it is most immediately determined by the daily movements in capital markets for the more or less uniform commodity which is money. But this market is the result of the most complex movements in the economy and as such cannot legitimately be used as a starting point for the analysis of the abstract determinants of production. Where the role played by money is absent in the labour market, it cannot be surreptitiously introduced into the capital market.

To criticize Shaikh is not to support his antagonists in the debate, for we have argued that both sides lie within the Okishian tradition. The reaction to Shaikh was necessarily to produce a hailstorm of alternative theories of the competitive behaviour of individuals and hence of the economy. Because the comparative statics of the Okishian theory already presumes a particular form of individual behaviour and competition to yield equilibrium, once out of equilibrium the analysis continues to be located at the level of individual motivation and necessarily conflicts with that necessary for equilibrium. How this is done is arbitrary from a theoretical point of view if not historically. Considerations such as expectations about prices or rates of interest reflect preoccupations with monopolization and the growth of the credit system. But these are simply tacked onto the theory and not incorporated adequately. For the Okishian theory, if the competitive tin of capitalist worms is left sealed, it can be safely assumed that they are all of the same size. Once it is opened, then there are any number of reasons why some might become fatter or longer than others.

Further Reading

For a survey of the debates over the LTRPF in greater detail, see Fine and Harris, *Rereading 'Capital'* (1979). The debate over the falling rate of profit in the *Cambridge Journal of Economics* took place in June 1978, December 1979 and March 1980. There are many popular accounts of Marx's LTRPF and they often seem to be derived from each other, to form a conventional wisdom that departs enormously from Marx's own presentation in Volume III of *Capital*. The original merits very careful reading.

9
Conclusions and Future Directions

In undertaking the research for this book, it became clear that there is much complexity and diversity in the ways in which various elements of understanding have been combined to produce the different theories of the capitalist economy. Throughout the book, these theories have been subject to careful scrutiny and criticism and have often been found to be wanting. Nevertheless, the conclusions to be drawn from the book are not unambiguously negative. We find that the tools necessary to understand the workings of the capitalist economy have long been available to economists even if they have only rarely been taken up and used with the necessary care and skill.

These remarks are particularly borne out by focusing on the contribution made by Adam Smith. It is worth rehearsing some of our findings in relation to his analysis. At the level of method, Smith saw underlying forces as governing the movement both between stages of development and within them. Conflicts between human propensities formed the basis for economic organization and the resolution of these conflicts gave rise to more definite and complex outcomes. This method enabled Smith to incorporate a significant historical and empirical content to his analysis even if not entirely to avoid the simple view of the economy as a model, however complex itself, running along and representing reality like a machine set in motion:

(Intellectual) systems in many respects resemble machines. A machine is a little system, created to perform as well as to connect together, in reality, those different movements and effects which the artist has occasion for. A system is an imaginary machine, invented to connect together in the fancy those different movements and effects which are already in reality performed (*Essays on Philosophical Subjects*, quoted in the introduction by Skinner to *The Wealth of Nations*, p. 12).

Smith's method also led him to utilize an understanding of the commercial stage based upon an analysis of the role of classes. This would appear to be inescapable for any theory that incorporates an historical element beyond the recognition that we live in a capitalist society. For the very form of revenues under capitalism, particularly of wages and profits, leads to an analysis based on class relations.

At the level of economic analysis itself, Smith himself immediately confronts the role played by the division of labour. Here the pin factory forms the starting point but it is also his point of departure from an analysis of the labour process. Whilst Smith recognizes the fate of the working class under a growing division of labour in production, it is an element that is soon abandoned in the elaboration of his theory. In addition, the consequences for capital of this developing division of labour in production are neglected by Smith. The coercive role played by competition in forcing accumulation of capital to obtain productivity increase is absent. In its place is the role played by the extent of the market in permitting such an accumulation. As a result, the conflict between the two classes over production becomes replaced by a belief in the possible harmony of expanding exchange relations in accommodating an increasing division of labour. Accordingly, it is not simply the absence of conflict over the division of labour in production that is notable in Smith but also the consequent absence of the implications of this for antagonisms within the exchange process itself. In other words, Smith implicitly raises the problem of the relationship between the division of labour in production and its division in exchange, only to give an absolute determining priority to the latter in limiting the extent of the former. By contrast, Marx did analyse the relationship between the two with a priority in determination to the division of labour in production (as we have shown in chapter 2). This in turn led to an analysis of the necessity of the centralization of capital and, accompanying it, the formation of a developed credit system. Consequently, exchange as such places no absolute barriers on the developing division of labour but nor does it permit its smooth evolution.

In his value analysis, Smith raises the labour theory of value, only again to take it as a point of departure for the subsequent analysis of price formation. The labour theory of value is limited in its application to the rude society where we can observe that no exchange would in any case be necessary. Again, Smith raises a problem that he has not properly answered: what are the conditions under which values as represented by labour time are formed? For Marx, the answer lies in a society of generalized commodity production, whereas for Smith and Ricardo the solution lies not in whether labour times are brought into equivalence with each other but whether they do so at prices that are proportional to labour values or not.

For Ricardo, whilst demonstrating the divergence between price and labour value, a commitment remains to the significance of labour time of production in determining price. This allows him to neglect some of the problems of value theory taken up by Smith in his components theory. As discussed in chapter 3, Ricardo simply recognized the problem of bringing labours exercised at different times into equivalence with each other and did so according to the principle of profits in proportion to capital advanced and for the length of time for which advances were made. Smith's components theory freed him from the necessity of bringing labours exercised at different times into equivalence with each other. It did, however, enable him to bring labours of different productivity into equivalence with each other, a problem that was absent from Ricardo except for his rent theory, and search for an invariable standard of value (to which we shall return below).

The way in which this is done by Smith is hidden by his use of the components theory which is based on wages, profits and rents rather than labour. As we have seen in chapter 5, Smith's components theory of wages and profits has them determined in part by the developing division of labour rather than exclusively by the static conditions associated with the present level of technology. This does indeed raise the question of the relationship between the current level and the developing level of productivity and how they are brought into equivalence through the market mechanism. Smith's own treatment is flawed by his skirting around the problem of raw materials whose value cannot be transformed by developing methods of production since they have already been produced. This leads Smith into a simple error that is criticized by Ricardo: an increase in wages cannot increase the price of all goods since the money commodity will itself have increased in price. But the simplicity of Smith's error and of Ricardo's criticism tends to conceal the problem of changing values with changing productivity that is Smith's object. Smith's reduction of the value of raw materials to a sequence of dated revenues parallels the Sraffian reduction of prices to dated and discounted wage payments. But where the Sraffians get it right (and Smith gets it wrong) is by leaving technology unchanged in the sequence of dates at which production takes place.

Smith's third component part of price is rent. Here, as we have argued in chapters 5 and 7, he constructs an absolute rent, as an addition to other costs, by confronting the free flow of capital onto the land with the barrier of landed property or a proxy for it. Here again, a contrast must be drawn with Ricardo, and it is a difference that is made possible by the historical perspective adopted by Smith. For Ricardo, it is axiomatic that capital flows freely onto the land (as demonstrated in chapter 4). The result is that rents are formed but quite independently of the system of landownership. Differential rents are formed to equalize the rate of profit in agriculture across lands of different fertility and location and these simply accrue to the landowners whomsoever they may be. A change of the system of landownership makes no difference since the rents simply pass to the new owners.

It can be seen that there is an intimate connection between the various parts of Smith's economic analysis: the components theory brings together the division of labour, the extent of the market and the role of landed property. For Marx, the same unity existed for the various elements of his theory, but the umbrella under which they sheltered was his value theory. Here there is an important contrast with Smith. The components theory of Smith developed in response to a recognition of the increasing complexity of exchange categories but it did so in immediate correspondence with those exchange categories themselves. The journey from the rude society to the commerical stage of capitalism saw the abondonment of a value theory based simply on labour and its replacement by the elements of capitalist costing: wages, profits and rents (but excluding raw materials).

In contrast, Marx examined how the complex categories of capitalist exchange corresponded to and reproduced the most simply conceived value relations based on labour time. After our discussion of Smith's contribution to economic analysis, we are in a position to see the problems posed for such a value theory of Marx. Once we move beyond the identification of Marx's value theory with Ricardo's as one of labour embodied, we recognize that in Marx's theory the formation of values represented the bringing into equivalence of different labours. Those labours are exercised in different sectors of the economy and for different capitals within sectors. Ricardo posed the problem of equivalence across industries with differing ratios of fixed to circulating capital and differing turnover times. In addition, we can observe that Ricardo tended to neglect the value of raw materials in establishing this equivalence. He also posed the problem of equivalence for differing productivities but only in the case of agriculture for which equivalence was established at the margin creating differential rents. Smith raised a different question: that of equivalence between labours of differing productivity as the division of labour develops. In doing so, he stumbled over the role played by raw materials: constant capital for Marx. Here is a capital whose value is preserved in production even as its value is being reduced by living labour as it increases productivity.

These various equivalences are problems for Marx's value theory, but the basis for their solution lies, like the justification of value theory itself, in the relations of commodity production. The source of the theoretical problems lies in the fact that these equivalences are established through exchange in its relationship to the accumulation of capital. The solutions can only be found by an examination of these relations rather than by an abandonment of value theory itself as suggested explicitly by Smith and the Sraffians, for example, and implicitly but reluctantly by Ricardo. In Marx's theory, the justification for and content of value theory lies in the equivalences established through the market between dead and living labour in different sectors with different levels of productivity. The market remains the means of establishing these equivalences but they are themselves derived from the conditions governing the accumulation of capital which is itself primarily a relationship of production between the two classes of capital and labour.

The significance of these remarks is borne out by Marx's theory of agricultural rent as presented in chapter 4. Here, the existence of absolute rent is recognized but only in the specific instances in which landed property forms an obstacle to the free flow of capital onto new land. The conditions in which value equivalence is established must therefore be examined.

Unquestionably, however, the bond that ties the various equivalences of labour together in Marx's theory is the role played by money. Exchange at a money price is the means by which the equivalences can be seen to have been established even as, paradoxically, the use of money conceals that it is different labours that are being brought into equivalence. For the equivalence is between commodities as things in so far as one dollar's worth of goods is considered equal to any other. In Marx's theory then the simple concept of value as created by labour is connected to the simple concept of money as its measure. But, in between there is to be accommodated the results of the accumulation of capital and its associated developments of the division of labour and class conflict. These connections have to be traced and it is at the most abstract level that Marx does this in his law of the tendency of the rate of profit to fall (see chapter 8). At a more concrete level, the workings of the law can only be understood through consideration of fixed capital and the more or less complex workings of the exchange system since money does not simply act as a means of payment but is itself integrated into a complex financial system. These problems are beyond the scope of the book but we have been able to see the issues that they raise and in particular the intimate connection between the production and formation of value and the role of money. For Ricardo, this problem proved a stumbling block in the futile search to obtain an invariable standard of value as technology changed. His approximate solution returned him to a labour theory of value but also created a divorce between production and exchange so that money played no significant role within his theory. Accordingly, movements in financial magnitudes could be examined in terms say of short term crises but they had no proper connection with the analysis of the 'real' economy.

In short, the tradition laid down by the authors considered immediately above is a rich and complex one. Necessarily it does not have immediate application to an understanding of contemporary capitalism because the economic principles involved are abstract. There is more work to be done as well as account to be taken of specific historical developments. At the time of writing, the world capitalist economy has been in a state of stagnation for almost a decade, and significant transformations have taken place in the economic role of the state, in the international nature of capital, and in the forms of money. The positive side to our conclusions here is that these developments can be confronted by a tradition that incorporates such diverse elements of analysis as have been presented.

But there is also a negative side. This is that the modern principles of economics have systematically and successfully excluded many of the elements of analysis that have been so advantageously present in the history of economic thought (as can be seen from chapters 6, 7 and 8). Model building has become the mark of the trade so that the economy is represented as an ideal machine running more or less successfully. But the result is to exclude any possible notion of the economy being embodied within a society with a history that distinguishes it from earlier stages of organization. The modern theory of production treats it simply as a technical relation between capital and labour in which both are things which combine to produce other things. How production develops as a social, let alone as an economic process, is only notable for its absence and this is most clear in the decline and disappearance of an explicit analysis of the division of labour. Value theory has been confined to a static equilibrium analysis in which the study of objective processes has been replaced by the aggregated effect of individual subjective preferences, in other words by utility theory. This in turn has left a residue of little or no distribution theory as wages, profits and rents are simply the prices of particular factor inputs. The presence of classes within the theory becomes negligible, they simply represent claims to revenue, the ownership of these various factors of production. This is demonstrated most clearly in the extinction of rent theory. From the time of Ricardo, there was no place for the effects of landed property on the formation of rent and the development of the economy. In modern times, there is not even a place for a specific theory of rent at all, and, if we are to be honest, nor for wages and profits.

The absence of a rent theory and of consideration of the division of labour are the most explicit instances showing what has been lost in the passage from classical political economy to the modern principles. What is absent from a theory can be as important in understanding it as in noticing what is present. The same considerations apply to theories concerning the falling rate of profit and their relation to crises. As we have seen, a debate exists within Marxist economics and it is one which raises many of the questions which we have highlighted above. Yet it is a debate that is more or less passed over by modern economics even if the principles of the latter can be shown to have infiltrated the debate. Instead, in the face of the crisis of world capitalism, a Keynesian orthodoxy persists (with a monetarism at one extreme) for which the most inappropriate economic principles will suffice. These are always pushing towards an individualized, disaggregated concept of the economy in which expectations, rational or otherwise, play the role as the only major theoretical concession to the changing economic and social environment. Political relations are simply conceived of as constraints within which the economist and the economy must work rather than as an element to be incorporated into the economic concepts themselves. Finally, empirical evidence is utilized in an increasingly sophisticated econometrics but again without this lending any conceptual content to the analysis concerned.

Let us return to Adam Smith. Whatever the drawbacks to his analysis in *The Wealth of Nations*, the questions raised there and the elements of analysis used to confront them must be faced. Our view is that this can be accomplished by a return to Marxist political economy and hopefully the reader has been persuaded of this where we have examined Marx's contribution to economic theory. Even so, the aim of this book has been slightly less ambitious. It has been to convince the reader of the necessity of a richer content to theories of the capitalist economy than can be found in the modern principles. If and when the rejection of these leads to the use of the principles of Marxist political economy, they still need to be brought to life in the light of contemporary capitalism. It is an exciting and challenging intellectual prospect.

References

ARMSTRONG, P. and GLYN, A. 1980: The Law of the Falling Rate of Profit and Oligopoly: A Comment on Shaikh. *Cambridge Journal of Economics*, Vol. 4, No. 1, pp. 69–70.

BERG, M. (ed.) 1979: *Technology and Toil in Nineteenth Century Britian*. London: CSE Books.

BLEANEY, M. 1980: Maurice Dobb's Theory of Crisis: A Comment. *Cambridge Journal of Economics*, Vol. 4, No. 1, pp. 71–4.

BOULDING, K. 1941: *Economic Analysis*. New York: Harper and Row.

—— 1945: The Concept of Economic Surplus. *American Economic Review*, XXXV, 4, pp. 851–69.

BRAVERMAN, H. 1974: *Labour and Monopoly Capital*. New York: Monthly Review Press.

BRENNER, R. 1977: The Origins of Capitalist Development: A Critique of Neo-Smithian Marxism. *New Left Review*, 104.

BROOME, J. 1977: Sraffa's Standard Commodity. *Australian Economic Papers*, Vol. 16, No. 29, pp. 231–6.

—— 1978: The Allegedly Invariable Value of Sraffa's Standard Commodity. *Birkbeck Discussion Paper*, 64.

BROWN, H. 1941: Economic Rent: In What Sense a Surplus? *American Economic Reivew*, XXXI, 4, pp. 833–5.

BUCHANAN, D. 1929: The Historical Approach to Rent and Price Theory. *Economica*, Vol. IX, No. 29, pp. 123–55.

CARLTON, F. 1906: The Relation of Marginal Rents to Price. *Quarterly Journal of Economics*, XX, pp. 596–607.

CLARK, J. 1891: Distribution as Determined by a Law of Rent. *Quarterly Journal of Economics*, V, pp. 289–318.

DOBB, M. 1973: *Theories of Value and Distribution since Adam Smith*. Cambridge: Cambridge University Press.

EDWARDS, R., REICH, M. and WEISSKOPF, T. 1972: *The Capitalist System: A Radical Analysis of American Society*. New York and Hemel Hempstead: Prentice Hall.

ELSON, D. (ed.) 1979: *Value: The Representation of Labour in Capitalism*. London: CSE Books.

FETTER, F. 1901: The Passing of the Old Rent Concept. *Quarterly Journal of Economics*, XV, pp. 416–55.

FINE, B. 1975: *Marx's 'Capital'*. London: Macmillan.

—— 1979: On Marx's Theory of Agricultural Rent. *Economy and Society*, Vol. 8, No. 3, pp. 241–78.

—— 1980: *Economic Theory and Ideology*. London: Edward Arnold. New York: Holmes and Meier.

—— 1981: Royalty or Rent: What's in a Name? *Birkbeck Discussion Paper*, 91.

FINE, B. and HARRIS, L. 1979: *Rereading 'Capital'*. London: Macmillan.

GREEN, F. and NORE, P. (eds.) 1977: *Economics: An Anti-Text*. London: Macmillan.

—— —— (eds.) 1979: *Issues in Political Economy*. London: Macmillan.

HARRIS, L. 1980: *Monetary Theory*. Maidenhead and New York: McGraw Hill.

HILTON, R. (ed.) 1976: *The Transition from Feudalism to Capitalism*. London: New Left Books.

HOBSON, J. 1891: The Law of the Three Rents. *Quarterly Journal of Economics*, V, pp. 263–88.

HOLLANDER, J. 1895: The Concept of Marginal Rent. *Quarterly Journal of Economics*, IX, pp. 175–87.

HOLLANDER, S. 1980: Post-Ricardian Dissension: A Case Study in Economics and Ideology. *Oxford Economic Papers*, Vol. 32, No. 3, pp. 370–410.

JEVONS, W. 1970: *The Theory of Political Economy*. Harmondsworth: Pelican.

LENIN, V. 1963: *Imperialism, The Highest Stage of Capitalism*, Selected Works Vol. I. Moscow: Progress Publishers.

MARSHALL, A. 1890: *Principles of Economics*. London: Macmillan.

—— 1893: On Rent. *Economic Journal*, III, pp. 74–90.

MARX, K. 1969: *Theories of Surplus Value* Part I. London: Lawrence and Wishart.

—— 1969: *Theories of Surplus Value* Part II. London: Lawrence and Wishart.

—— 1972: *Capital* Volume III. London: Lawrence and Wishart.

—— 1976: *Capital* Volume I. Harmondsworth: Penguin.

MEEK, R. 1962: *The Economics of Physiocracy: Essays and Translations*. London: Allen and Unwin.

—— and SKINNER, A. 1973: The Development of Adam Smith's Ideas on the Division of Labour. *Economic Journal*, 83, pp. 1094–116.

MISHAN, E. 1959: Rent as a Measure of Welfare Change. *American Economic Review*, XLIX. 3, pp. 386–95.

—— 1968: What is Producers' Surplus? *American Economic Review*, LVIII, 5.1, pp. 1269–82.

—— 1969: Rent and Producers Surplus: Reply. *American Economic Review*, LIX, 4.1, pp. 635–7.

NAKATANI, T. 1980: The Law of the Falling Rate of Profit and Oligopoly: Comment on Shaikh. *Cambridge Journal of Economics*, Vol. 4, No. 1, pp. 65–8.

OKISHIO, N. 1961: Technical Change and the Rate of Profit. *Kobe University Economic Review*, 7, pp. 85–99.

PARIJS, P. VAN. 1980: The Falling-Rate-of-Profit Theory of Crisis: A Rational Reconstruction by Way of Obituary. *Review of Radical Politcal Economy*, 12.1, pp. 1–16.

RICARDO, D. 1951: *Principles of Political Economy and Taxation* with an introduction by Sraffa, P., volume I to *Works*. Cambridge: Cambridge University Press.

—— 1951: *Works*, ed. in eleven volumes by Sraffa, P. Cambridge: Cambridge University Press.

ROEMER, J. 1979: Continuing Controversy on the Falling Rate of Profit and Other Issues. *Cambridge Journal of Economics*, Vol. 3, No. 4, pp. 379–98.

SHAIKH, A. 1978: Political Economy and Capitalism: Notes on Dobb's Theory of Crisis. *Cambridge Journal of Economics*, Vol. 2, No. 2, pp. 233–51.

—— 1980: Marxian Competition versus Perfect Competition: Further Comments on the so-called Choice of Technique. *Cambridge Journal of Economics*, Vol. 4, No. 1, pp. 75–83.

SMITH, A. 1976: *The Theory of Moral Sentiments*. Ed. by Raphael, D. and Macfie, A. Oxford: Oxford University Press.

—— 1970: *The Wealth of Nations*. Harmondsworth: Pelican.

SRAFFA, P. 1969: *Production of Commodities by Means of Commodities*. Cambridge: Cambridge University Press.

STEEDMAN, I. 1980: A Note on the 'Choice of Technique' under Capitalism. *Cambridge Journal of Economics*, Vol. 4, No. 1, pp. 61–4.

WALRAS, L. 1954: *Elements of Pure Economics* (a translation of the *Edition Definitive* (1926)). Homewood, Illinois: Richard D. Irwin.

WESSEL, R. 1967: A Note on Economic Rent. *American Economic Review*, LVII. 5, pp. 1221–26.

—— 1969: What is Producers' Surplus? – Comment. *American Economic Review*, LIX, 4.1, pp. 634–5.

Index